About the author

Pamela Cunnington was an architect in private practice and
for seventeen years the Historic Buildings Officer for the
county of Dorset. She was a Lethaby Scholar of the Society
for the Protection of Ancient Buildings, and a NADFAS
Church Recorder. Her books on domestic architecture are
well known, and her life-long interest in church buildings
makes *How Old is That Church?* a natural successor to her
much praised *How Old is Your House?* and *Care for Old
Houses*. She died in 1993.

How Old is That Church?

Pamela Cunnington

Photographs by Peter Burton,
Harland Walshaw
and the author

Marston House

© The estate of Pamela Cunnington 1993

Designed and produced by Alphabet & Image Ltd, Sherborne, Dorset DT9 3LU.

Published by Marston House, Marston Magna, Yeovil BA22 8DH

First Published 1990, revised edition published 1993

British Library Cataloguing in Publication Data
A catalogue record for this book is available from the British Library.

ISBN 0 9517700 9 8

Acknowledgements
The author would like to thank the following for their help in the preparation of Chapter 15: Mr D.I. Findlay of the Council for the Care of Churches, Mrs Jennifer Demolder of the Liturgy Office of the Catholic Bishops' Conference of England and Wales, and Mr R.J. Morris of the Council for British Archaeology (Chapels' Society). The photographs in this book are by Peter Burton and Harland Walshaw, with the exception of the following: Alphabet & Image Ltd, p.116; M. Breach, 175; Pamela Cunnington, 13, 15b, 18, 20, 23, 24, 37, 38, 39, 41, 42l, 46, 49, 57, 58, 65, 68, 69, 77t, 79, 86l, 89, 93, 95, 98, 102, 111, 112, 114, 122, 123, 125, 126, 127, 129, 133, 136b, 144, 146, 147, 148, 149, 150, 151, 155, 156, 158, 162 (courtesy Mr Somerset de Chair), 164, 165t, 166, 168, 170, 172, 173r, 179, 181, 183b, 187, 194, 195, 198, 207, 209, 214tr, 214br, 214bl, 216, 234, 235, 236; Faber & Faber, 108l (Plate VI, from an engraving in *A Course of Catechising* etc; second edition 1674) and 108r (Plate I, The Communion Service, from the frontispiece to the second edition of C. Wheatly, *A Rational Illustration of the Book of Common Prayer*; 1714) both published in Addleshaw & Etchells *The Architectural Setting of Anglican Worship*; S. Grose Hodge, 128; C. McVean, 1731; J. Mennell, 157; G. Wheeler, 197. All line drawings are by the author.

Front cover: St Mary's, Breamore, Hants, an important and large Saxon cruciform church with later additions. Back cover: St Mary's, Fairford, Glos., a wool merchants' church of the fifteenth century.

Printed in Great Britain by The Bath Press, Bath, Avon.

Contents

Foreword

Shortly before her death in May 1993, Pamela Cunnington had finished the revisions for the new edition of "How Old is that Church?", but sadly she did not live to see its realisation. The author has bequeathed the royalties from the book to the Society for the Protection of Ancient Buildings, in a generous gesture typical of her thoughtfulness. Some of Pamela's fellow members, colleagues and friends pay tribute to her in this foreword to the new edition.

Pamela's love of history and architecture, in particular that of English parish churches, was probably first awakened during her childhood by her grandfather's enthusiasm for ecclesiology. So, on leaving school in 1942, she determined to become an architect – an unusual choice of career for a woman at that time. She completed her training, gaining a distinction in 1949 for her final examination thesis; its title – 'The Development of Modern Church Design' – is an indication that her interest in church buildings had continued and deepened as she grew up.

Practical training in the care of old buildings followed in 1950, when Pamela was awarded one of the Lethaby scholarships offered by the SPAB to newly-qualified young architects. In common with the majority of scholars from other years, she found the six-month course an invaluable experience, fundamental to specialisation in this field. The opportunity to spend time discussing the various approaches to problems of decay, while acquiring understanding of materials and repair techniques through on-site work all over the country, was unusual for that period. It still has a unique quality, related to its emphasis on the philosophy of repair expressed by the Society's founder, William Morris, in his *Manifesto* of 1877, which profoundly influenced Pamela's attitude towards conservation methods throughout her life.

Fellow scholars of the 1950s remember Pamela's quiet concentration and thoroughness in producing neat and accurate measured drawings. Her self-effacing manner hid a dry sense of humour which in the company of friends could be teased into the open. Soon after finishing the Lethaby scholarship, she began conducting her own practice from London, working on many historic buildings both domestic and ecclesiastical. Later she became the Historic Buildings Officer for Dorset County Council and, after her retirement in 1986, continued to make her home in Dorchester for the rest of her life.

Colleagues have remarked on her eye for archaeological detail, and exceptional talent for unravelling the historical and architectural development of a building. House owners became enthused as Pamela explained the significance of some detail of construction, revealed perhaps during her close examination of a roof space or under-floor area, and were gently encouraged to take appropriate action in caring for their property. On the other hand, in defending historic buildings against applications for demolition, unacceptable alterations or additions, her steely determination surprised many developers as she overcame their arguments and withstood commercial pressure. During the latter part of her life, she shared the full range of her interest and experience with others, as leader of guided walks, or through lectures given with a simple but effective delivery. Between 1980 and 1988 she produced three books on domestic architecture and its conservation.

In the last of her books, *How Old is that Church?*, published in 1990, Pamela Cunnington returned to the central interest of her life, begun as a child's hobby but developing into a serious study in adulthood. Opportunities to augment her research may have occurred over the years during professional visits made to churches undergoing building work, but the book is not a manual for repairs to their fabric. It is a straightforward account of the development of church building in Britain, well organised, beautifully illustrated and including both a glossary of architectural terms and a useful list of bodies concerned with churches at the present time. Written with the clarity of style characteristic of the author, it will provide an answer to all those who have ever asked the question in the title.

The Society for the Protection of Ancient Buildings is proud to be associated with the publication of this new edition of *How Old is that Church?*

Peter and Janet Locke
for the Society for the Protection of Ancient Buildings

1

Introduction and sources

England is fortunate in its parish churches. Other countries may have grander cathedrals and abbeys, but few can show such a fine collection of parish churches, in villages and towns, as those of this country. The main reason is perhaps obvious. Because of our island situation we have suffered less than most other European countries from the devastation of war, and although, as we shall see, the Church of England has passed through many upheavals which have affected the furnishing and internal arrangement of churches, far less damage has been done to the actual structures than has happened elsewhere. This book is concerned primarily with parish churches, although we must remember that most new architectural developments began in the greater churches — the cathedrals and larger abbeys — and filtered down to the parishes, where they were modified to suit the local needs and resources.

When we visit an old town or village and want to find out something of its history, it is natural to make first for the church, especially if it is an early one, or one on an old site. The church, being probably the oldest and most permanent building in the place, can tell us much about its history, and not only its exclusively ecclesiastical history; for the hard and fast division between the sacred and the secular that we take for granted today is something comparatively recent. In the medieval period, and for some centuries to follow, the church, with the manor house near which it is often found, was the focal point of the community.

The changes which have taken place in our churches, like those in our houses, have reflected not only the changes in architectural styles and fashions, but changes in population and economic prosperity and,

St Peter's Church, Petersham, Greater London. *The outside view of this largely brick-built church close to Richmond in Surrey gives little idea of the riches to be found inside. A small thirteenth-century church, it was largely rebuilt and refurnished in the late eighteenth century. It escaped Victorian restoration and contains box pews painted dark red, an elegant pulpit, and a combined reading pew and clerk's desk. The altar, in the tiny sanctuary, is almost hidden behind these furnishings, but the Jacobean wall tomb can clearly be seen.*

9

perhaps most important, changes in the way they have been used, that is, in the forms of public worship, and the part played by the church in the life of the parish. Churches have not only been used for worship. In the Middle Ages, and to some extent up to the eighteenth century, they were used for certain secular purposes. A survival of this custom may be seen in the way some civil notices are still fixed to the church door, or in the porch. The modern dual-purpose church-cum-hall probably has more in common with its medieval predecessors than is generally appreciated.

The dating of churches is made more difficult by the fact that any building which has been in use for many centuries will almost certainly have been altered many times. Occasionally we will find an almost completely unaltered Norman church, or, rather more often, one rebuilt in the prosperous years of the late fifteenth century and little altered since, but these are the exceptions. In most cases churches will have been altered, enlarged, or occasionally reduced in size to suit the conditions of their day, and, as we shall see, this is a continuing process.

Anyone wanting to make a serious study of the history of a church, for instance in order to write a church guide book, will, in addition to looking for the architectural evidence, want to make use of any documentary evidence available. It will be found that parishes vary considerably in the amount of their surviving material. For the early medieval period it will be necessary to consult such documents as taxation and valuation returns, and the bishops' registers. These may be available for inspection either in the Diocesan Registry, or in the County Record Office. Perhaps we should note at this stage that whereas the mention of a church in the *Domesday Book* indicates that one existed in that parish at that time, the lack of such a mention does not necessarily mean that no church existed there. The *Domesday Book* was compiled to facilitate taxation, and churches were not normally taxable.

Where, as we shall see later, parish churches came under the control of religious houses, the monastic records (which may also be available in the Diocesan or County Record Office) may give details of the building, rebuilding or alterations of the parish churches for which they were responsible. All these early records are likely to be in Latin, and in an early script which may not be easy to decipher, but sometimes they will have been transcribed into modern English by a local historical society. From the later medieval period onwards, more information may be found in the churchwardens' accounts, which can include amounts of money paid to masons, carpenters and other craftsmen for work to the church, as well as such items as money given for the relief of the poor, and the bounties paid for killing vermin!

The vestry minutes may also include items referring to building repairs and alterations, and sometimes the reports of the proceedings of the church courts can provide not only information about the church, but also an insight into parish life. These may still be with the parish, but will often have been deposited in the County Record Office. The Diocesan Record Office may have information relating to particular parishes, including the bishops' and archdeacons' Visitations. These comment on the condition of the church, the need for repairs, and note whether work recommended in the previous Visitation has been carried out. The Diocesan Record Office should also have copies of all Faculties (i.e. permits granted by the Diocesan Chancellor to carry out work to the church or its furnishings). These, particularly in the eighteenth, nineteenth and twentieth centuries, were often accompanied by drawings showing the work.

Parish magazines from the nineteenth century onwards can be a fruitful source of information about church building work, as can local newspapers (to be found in the local reference library). These can give interesting accounts of commemorative services at the completion of a restoration, and may well include details such as the cost of the work and the names of the architect and the builder. The library should also be able to provide local histories, such as the *Victoria County Histories*, or the transactions of local historical or antiquarian societies which may throw light on the history of the church.

All this research is likely to take a considerable time, and the average church visitor, for whom this book is primarily intended, will probably have to depend mainly on the architectural evidence provided by the building, although many churches have a printed guide book or history, the standard of most of which has improved much in recent years.

Apart from what the building can tell us as it stands, new evidence may well be provided by archaeology, although it is only rarely possible to carry out a full archaeological investigation of a church still in use. More often these discoveries are made almost by accident, arising from alteration works such as the renewal of floors, or the digging of drainage trenches. It is therefore important to see that all such works are carefully monitored to avoid the loss of important historical evidence.

In the next few chapters we shall be looking at the development of church design and furnishing from the introduction of Christianity to this country until the present time.

All Saint's, Earl's Barton, Northants.

2

Saxon

Let us start by looking at the first evidence for Christianity in England. We know that the Christian faith reached Britain during the period of the Roman occupation. In AD314, two years after Christianity became the official religion of the Roman Empire, two British bishops attended the Council of Arles, indicating that the Church must have been established well before that date. One of the earliest pieces of evidence for Romano-British Christianity has been revealed at Lullingstone Roman Villa, Kent (the inspiration for R.C. Sheriff's play *The Long Sunset*) where, from evidence of wall paintings, a room was apparently used as a Christian chapel in about AD350. Then we have the mosaic pavement, incorporating Christian symbols, found in a Roman villa excavated at Hinton Saint Mary, Dorset, and probably also dating from the fourth century. At this time Christian worship would have been held mainly in private houses, as the number of Christians in any district would rarely justify the building of a church, except in the larger centres of population.

No Romano-British churches survive above ground today, unless we accept Saint Martin's Church, Canterbury, as being of this period, but we may assume that they followed the basilican form found elsewhere in the Roman Empire. These churches derived their plan from that of the secular basilica — a public hall found in almost all Roman Towns — which served the purposes of meeting hall and law courts. The typical basilican church consisted of an aisled hall, or nave, with a semi-circular apsidal sanctuary at one end, divided from the nave by a wide semi-circular arch, or sometimes by a triple arch, forming a type of screen. The central nave, rising higher than the aisles, was lit by high-level clerestory windows. Sometimes there were shallow transepts at the junction of the nave and the sanctuary to provide space for ceremonial, and at the end of the nave furthest from the sanctuary was either a covered porch, or an open courtyard, or both, this part of the church being called the narthex. The altar stood in the centre of the apse, and in front of it was an enclosed space for the choir, surrounded by low screens. The influence of this early church plan can be seen in most medieval cathedrals and larger abbeys.

The foundations of what was probably a small church have been uncovered at the Roman town of Silchester, near Reading, and this shows all these features on a small scale, indicating the type of church likely to have been built in an outlying province of the Empire.

After the Roman legions withdrew from Britain in the fifth century Christianity almost disappeared in much of the country, although there is some evidence for its survival among the Britons in Ireland, Wales and Cornwall. This survival may have been more widespread than was once thought. In the Church of Lady Saint Mary, Wareham, Dorset, a series of inscribed stones indicates the continuation of British Christianity after the Saxon conquest. A revival of church building in England, however, had to wait until the Christian faith was established among the Saxons.

The conversion of Saxon England was carried out by two distinct agencies: the Celtic missionaries from Ireland whose influence was felt most in the north and west of the country, and the Roman mission under Augustine which began in Kent, spreading out from there, first influencing the south and east. The boundaries between the spheres of influence were not clear-cut; there was a certain amount of overlapping, and, indeed, rivalry and dissent before the two missions eventually combined, after the Synod of Whitby AD664, to form the Church of England. These influences seem to be reflected in the designs of the earlier Saxon churches, which were of two distinct forms.

The churches built as a result of the Roman mission show, as we might expect, the influence of the basilican plan, though in a simplified form.

Typical Roman (basilican) Saxon church plan

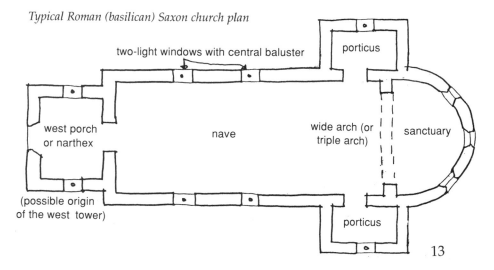

two-light windows with central baluster

porticus

west porch
or narthex

nave

wide arch (or
triple arch)

sanctuary

(possible origin
of the west tower)

porticus

St Peter's Church, Bradwell-on-Sea, Essex was built over the site of a Roman fort, incorporating re-used Roman brick, and is the surviving nave of a basilican-type church. The sanctuary, western narthex and porticus have gone, but evidence for them can still be seen. The large built-up opening in the side wall was a cart entrance, formed when the building was used as a barn.

Generally, except for a few major churches such as that at Brixworth, Northamptonshire, they were not aisled. The typical church of this group was rectangular in plan, with a shallow apsidal sanctuary as wide, or nearly as wide, as the nave, and divided from it by a wide, high arch, or by a triple arch. There were often transepts, or lateral porches, and sometimes a western porch or narthex. Some larger churches had, instead of the typical basilican aisles, a series of continuous attached porches, or transepts, called porticus, along each side of the nave. These were perhaps used as chapels, or burial places, and were sometimes later additions to an earlier, unaisled, nave.

One of the earliest surviving churches of this type can be seen at Bradwell-on-Sea, Essex, dating, it is believed, from AD653. The apse and the transepts have vanished, but traces of them can still be seen, together with parts of a western narthex and the built-up triple arches which led into the apse. This church also illustrates the re-use of Roman bricks by the Saxons; in this case from a fort, on the site of which the church was built.

14

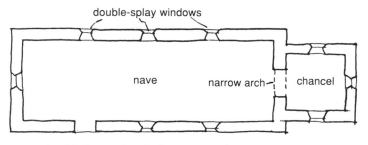

Typical Celtic Saxon church plan

The other basic form of early Saxon church is quite different, and it is difficult to see how it could have been derived from the basilican plan. These churches, of which the best surviving examples are at Escombe in County Durham, and Bradford-on-Avon in Wiltshire, consist of a rectangular aisle-less nave and a narrower rectangular chancel, linked by a very narrow chancel arch. Like the basilican churches they may have transepts or porticus, but these, like the chancel, are entered from the nave by narrow arches or doorways. Such churches form, in effect, a series of separate rooms, and they are generally very high in relation to their length and breadth. From their general distribution it would seem that they owe their form to the influence of the Celtic, rather than the Roman, mission. Various theories have been advanced about the origin of this type of Saxon church, but the one put forward by the late W. Croome, in lectures given for the Council for the Care of Churches (based, I believe, on those of the late Edward Cutts in his book *The Parish Priest and his People*) would seem to have something to recommend it, since it may help to explain certain features peculiar to the Church in England which might otherwise be hard to understand.

To start with, we need to look at the way the Christian faith was propagated in Saxon England. In selected areas, generally in towns or large villages, a fairly large church was built, known as a 'Minster', served by several priests who might or might not be monks. The term 'Minster' does not necessarily mean a monastery, but any large church. York Minster, for example, was not monastic but served by secular clergy. Some of the original minster churches were, or later became, cathedrals, but since the dioceses of that period were very large they were served by additional minsters, which eventually became parish churches. They can sometimes be recognised today by the element 'minster' in the place name.

From the minster church, or mission station, priests went out to the surrounding villages to preach the Gospel, at first preaching in the open air. The stone crosses found in some towns and villages may mark the

sites of these first mission services. Free-standing crosses of this type are found in Ireland, and this tradition could well have been continued by the Celtic missionaries. Later, according to Mr Croome's theory, if the priest was accepted he might build himself a small hut, or chapel. This would probably be of wood, similar to the homes of the villages, but perhaps distinguished by having a cross fixed above the doorway in one end wall. Here the priest would build an altar and say Mass. This simple form of church was, like the standing crosses, common in Ireland where early monastic life, though strict, was not lived communally like that on the Continent and in medieval England, and thus did not produce large monastic churches.

As the priest gained converts among the villagers, they would gather around the open door of the chapel to watch him, and try to follow the services. As pagans they were used to worshipping in the open air, but after they had been baptised and become members of the Church, able to take a full part in its services, they would no longer be content to assemble 'outside' the church and would build themselves a covered annexe, or 'nave', to the west of the original chapel, which then became

LEFT *A tenth-century carved shaft (possibly a cross-shaft), now in the undercroft of York Minster.* BELOW *Part of a carved frieze in SS Mary and Hardulph's Church, Breedon-on-the-Hill, Leics. The symbolism of these strange animal figures is unclear, but they are believed to date from the eighth century.*

the 'chancel'. The original doorway thus became the chancel arch, and the wooden cross over it developed into the Rood — the large crucifix flanked by figures of Saint Mary and Saint John, which became a feature of every medieval church. Interestingly, this early development seems to have been repeated at a later date at Canford Magna Church, Dorset, Here the original Saxon minster church is now the chancel, to which the Norman builders added an aisled nave.

Returning to the early Saxon wooden church; since the nave had been built by the parishioners it remained their property, and they were responsible for its repair, while the chancel remained the responsibility of the mission priest, and the rector who succeeded him once the church had become established and the village had become the nucleus of a parish. This was the case until comparatively recent times, when tithes were abolished, and even today there are some churches where there is a lay rector, responsible for the chancel repairs, a development which will be explained in a later chapter.

Tithes, a tenth of all produce from the parishioners' crops and animals,

18

were the means by which the parish priest or rector lived. He also held land, known as glebe, probably given him by the local thegn or landowner, which he originally farmed himself but later usually let out for rent. Often the church is found near the manor house, indicating that the thegn took the mission priest under his protection, gave him the land for his chapel, and employed him as his chaplain.

Since the church nave had been built by the parishioners, they felt entitled to use it for purposes other than worship. Throughout the medieval period, and later, churches served also as village halls, being used for meetings and various social purposes. As the most substantial building in the parish the church could also be used as a place of refuge in times of danger, and in areas subject to flooding it will be found on the highest available ground.

The ruined church at Knowlton, Dorset. This church stands in the centre of a Neolithic henge monument, and may represent a deliberate attempt to 'take over' a pre-Christian religious site.

To protect the chancel — the holy place of the Mass — from profane use, it eventually became usual to erect a screen across the chancel arch, solid at the bottom and with open tracery above. In the centre were gates, closed except during service time. The screen thus corresponds to the movable partition, shutting off the sanctuary, found in some modern dual-purpose churches.

After the Synod of Whitby (AD664) the two branches of the Church combined to form the Church of England, and officially the Roman influence predominated. This clearly affected the design of the later Saxon churches, but certain elements of the Celtic tradition survived. The narrow chancel arch gave way to a wider one, but the chancels were often longer — not simply apsidal sanctuaries — and they were sometimes square-ended, a British tradition which also survived the next wave of continental influence after the Norman conquest. The tall, narrow proportions of the Celtic-type church also survived. In some churches, such as that at Deerhurst, Gloucestershire, certain door and window openings at high level in the west wall of the nave suggest that there were sometimes upper floors, or galleries, in these churches. Whether the

St Mary's Church, Deerhurst, Glos. Only a short distance from Odda's Chapel, this important Saxon church contains much of interest. The tall proportions, and the doorway and windows leading from the tower into the upper part of the nave suggest that there may have been a gallery or upper floor. The triangular-headed Saxon windows are probably derived from timber construction. The tower arch is also Saxon, but the nave arcades are thirteenth-century.

ABOVE *Escombe Church, County Durham. This important Saxon church shows the tall, narrow proportions of the Celtic-type plan. Note the long and short quoins, and the small window with its head cut from a single stone. The other windows in this wall are later insertions.* LEFT *St Mary's Church, Sompting, Sussex. The well-known Saxon tower of this church retains an interesting 'Rhenish' helm capping, still covered in oak shingles. Note also the pilaster strips, and the paired belfry windows.*

upper rooms were used for worship or, perhaps, as living accommodation for the clergy, cannot now be determined.

Towers were features of the more important Saxon churches, and probably originated as look-outs and defensive structures. Sometimes a central tower is found, between the nave and the chancel, and where this is flanked by porticus it produces a cruciform plan more typical of the Norman period. Unlike Norman and medieval churches of this plan form, though, in Saxon churches the nave, chancel and porticus are generally narrower than the tower, leaving exposed external angles — sometimes a useful factor in dating a church to this period. In other churches, towers were at the west end, and this was eventually to become the normal practice in England. In a few cases, such as Earls Barton, Northamptonshire, the large tower rises above the nave itself.

23

St Nicholas' Church, Worth, Sussex. The chancel arch, and those leading to the porticus, are of typical Saxon form. The width of the chancel arch suggests Roman, rather than Celtic influence. In the apse are three deeply splayed windows.

Worth Church, Sussex, restored in 1989 after fire damage which destroyed the Victorian roof, follows the basilican plan form, but its tall proportions indicate Celtic influence. It is one of the most complete Saxon churches surviving in England, the Victorian tower being the only substantial addition.

The first Saxon churches were mainly of timber, and one of these has survived, at Greenstead-by-Ongar, Essex. Though much restored it retains its original external walls of split logs, laid vertically. Some Saxon stone churches show the influence of timber construction, perhaps indicating that their builders were more used to building in timber than in stone. The typical Saxon detailing at the quoins (vertical angles of the building), known as 'long and short' work, is quite illogical as masonry construction. It is probably an ornamental feature derived from timber framing, as is the surface patterning with pilaster strips of ashlar stone, found on some Saxon walling, including towers. The rough rubble stone walling between these strips was probably plastered, producing a finished appearance reminiscent of timber-framed construction. In

RIGHT *St Peter's Church, Barton-on-Humber, Humberside. The western narthex and splendid tower are Saxon, and display pilaster strips in an ornamental pattern (perhaps derived from timber-framing). Note also the triangular and round-headed paired windows. The lower walls of the tower retain their plastered finish.*

24

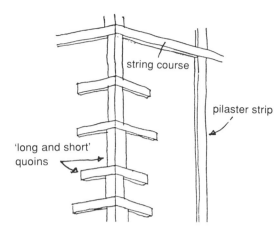

string course

pilaster strip

'long and short' quoins

Two-light triangular-headed window

Plan

Saxon walling details. The long and short quoins and pilaster strips project in front of the rubble walling, to take a plastered finish.

Triangular-headed Saxon windows, as above, would originally have been unglazed.

windows and doorways the triangular heads, so typical of Saxon work, are probably derived from timber construction, as is the use of turned stone balusters dividing pairs of unglazed windows. Herringbone masonry is found in Saxon walling, but it is not necessarily a sign of Saxon date, as its use continued after the Norman conquest.

All the surviving Saxon churches have since been re-roofed, but they probably had simple timber roofs, covered with thatch or wood shingles. Saxon chancel and tower arches and doorways are generally semi-circular, often rather plain, with 'imposts' or projecting stones at their springing, perhaps a simplification of the classical capital. A free adaptation of classical carving is sometimes found, as are grotesque animal heads, harking back to Celtic, or perhaps reflecting Scandinavian influence. Round-headed windows, the arch cut from a single stone, are sometimes splayed both internally and externally. Indeed, an external splay is nearly always an indication of Saxon date.

Saxon fonts were large enough to allow for baptism by total immersion, and were typically of the 'tub' form, tapering towards the base. They may be quite plain, or decorated, often with interlaced designs.

The Saxon architectural details I have described should help us to recognise work of this period, and the Saxon origin of a building which has seen many later alterations. Indeed, several changes may have taken place during the Saxon period itself, which lasted for over 400 years — as long as the period between the Norman conquest and the accession of the Tudors — and during this time increasing contact with the rest of Europe must have influenced the design of churches. It is easy to forget, though, that even the least altered Saxon church that we can find today would

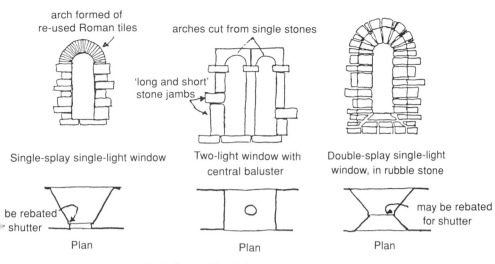

arch formed of re-used Roman tiles

arches cut from single stones

'long and short' stone jambs

Single-splay single-light window

Two-light window with central baluster

Double-splay single-light window, in rubble stone

be rebated shutter

Plan

Plan

may be rebated for shutter

Plan

Typical round-headed Saxon window details

have looked very different to a member of its original congregation, and this would be true for much of the medieval period. The Saxon worshipper would not, for a start, have approached his church through a churchyard filled with tombstones. Anyone wealthy enough to afford a monument would have been buried inside the church. In the churchyard the south side was more favoured for burials, the north side being popularly associated with the Devil. In old churchyards the ground on the south side of the church can often be found to be higher than that on

LEFT *The Saxon font at St Mary's Church, Deerhurst, Glos*

27

the north, irrespective of any natural fall in the ground, having been built up by repeated burials.

The walls of early churches, if built of rubble stone or flint, were generally plastered, and limewashed inside and out. Inside, the walls were often painted, either marked out in red lines to imitate ashlar stone, or with pictorial scenes from the Bible or the lives of the saints. The stripping of this plaster to expose rubble stone was a bad Victorian practice, still popular today in some places, and it has resulted in the loss of much early painted decoration. The stone dressings to door and window openings would also have been coloured in with the plaster. Over the chancel arch, or above the screen in medieval churches, was the Rood. Behind this, on a lath and plaster partition known as a tympanum, filling the upper part of the chancel arch, there was generally a painted representation of the Last Judgement.

The floor would probably have been of beaten earth, covered with rushes. Only the richer churches at this early period would have had stone floors. There would have been no seating in the nave; people stood, knelt, or sat on the floor during the services. Services were shorter than they are today, and as sermons were rare, pulpits had not yet appeared. The only fixture in the nave would have been the font, set near the principal door. In the chancel would have been the altar, of stone, covered during service time with a frontal. On it would be two candles and probably a cross. The candles were necessary to enable the priest to read, and not merely ceremonial features as they are today. There would have been little seating in the chancel, no choirstalls, but probably one row of seats on each side. These would be for the priest, the parish clerk, and a few singing boys who also acted as servers. These seats were sometimes

A Saxon corbel in Deerhurst Church, showing a carved animal head.

The tall Saxon polygonal apse to the sanctuary at All Saints' Church, Wing, Bucks. Note the ornamental pilaster strips and Saxon windows at high level. The lower windows are later medieval insertions. The walling was probably originally plastered.

part of the structure, simple stone benches set into the walls. Those on the south side, for the clergy, and known as sedilia, became in later medieval times quite ornate. Also in later medieval times some seats were 'returned', backing on to the screen, facing east, for use by the clergy taking the offices of matins and evensong.

General artificial lighting in the church would have been from candles or rushlights. No great concentration of light was needed in the nave. Few of the people could read, and all that was required was sufficient light for them to see their way in, and follow the actions of the priest at Mass. In any case, true evening services were rare. Evensong would have been at about 3 p.m. Heating, if it existed at all, was probably by charcoal braziers. The small Saxon windows were unglazed, and fitted with wooden shutters which could be closed against the wind. Glass, which was very expensive at this time, was probably fitted first into the chancel.

The siting of the church in relation to the village shows some interesting variations. In some cases a central position was chosen. As previously mentioned, we often find the church close to the manor house, since in Saxon times the rector was usually appointed by the thegn, or principal landowner. The manor boundaries generally became those of the parish, which was both a civil and an ecclesiastical unit, but a parish might sometimes comprise more than one small manor. There is some evidence of churches being built on pre-Christian religious sites. This was probably a deliberate decision, in view of the strong religious associations of such sites and the fear that converts might slip back into the old ways. In the same way the old pagan feasts were transformed into Christian festivals, such as Christmas, Easter, Saint John the Baptist's Day (Midsummer), and All Saints' Day (1st November, the start of winter).

Towards the end of the Saxon period the influence of Norman and other continental Romanesque architecture began to appear in England, which was becoming less isolated from the rest of Europe. The later Saxon cathedrals and abbeys seem to have been substantial stone aisled buildings, and although they were practically all rebuilt after the Norman conquest, more evidence of their design is being revealed by archaeological investigation. It is now believed, for instance, that the apparently Norman nave of Sherborne Abbey, Dorset, is in fact a Saxon structure, partly remodelled after the conquest, and when King Edward the Confessor built Westminster Abbey, London, the result was, in effect, a Norman building. On the other hand, certain features regarded as typically Saxon may be found in early Norman churches, which must have been built by Saxon workmen, especially in the villages. It is therefore not always easy, in the absence of documentary evidence to say whether a church, or parts of it, definitely date from before or after the conquest. As will be explained in the next chapter, though, great changes were to take place at that time, inevitably affecting church architecture.

In spite of the fact that physical evidence for Saxon work in churches is far less than that for later periods (although more Saxon features are continually being discovered), I have dealt with the period at some length. It represents a long period in our history, and it was during this time that many of the principles of medieval church design evolved, from the fusion of the Roman basilican plan with the native Celtic plan. The resulting, typically English church plan was to survive the next influx of continental ideas. The fact that much evidence for Saxon, and indeed other early work in a church is often uncovered during repairs and alterations illustrates the need for great care in carrying out such work.

Holy Trinity Church, Great Paxton, Cambs. This late Saxon church already shows signs of the influence of the Norman Romanesque style in the arcade capitals.

3

Norman

The Norman conquest in 1066-7 affected the whole civil structure of England, bringing great changes to the Church and, as a result, to church architecture. As we have seen, the first signs of this became apparent before the actual conquest, notably in the work of King Edward at Westminster, and it is interesting to speculate on the possible course of English church design, and indeed of the whole of English culture, if Harold had won at Hastings.

In the event, though, the control and running of the Church was taken over by the Normans who, although of Norse stock, had been settled in France for long enough to have assimilated a continental outlook on most matters. Most of the Saxon bishops and many parish priests were replaced by Normans who almost immediately started on a programme of church reform which included much rebuilding. In effect, nearly all the Saxon cathedrals and abbeys were rebuilt, as were most of the parish churches. Although the Norman period of architecture was much shorter than the preceding Saxon period, far more evidence of their work has survived until today.

In some cases the actual sites of the cathedrals were moved, as part of the Norman policy of bringing the Church more closely under the control of the civil authorities. The sees — the seats of the bishops — were therefore sometimes transferred to the principal towns of the area. In this way the Saxon cathedral of Selsey, Sussex, was demolished and replaced by a new building at Chichester, and that at Thetford, Norfolk, replaced by one at Norwich. In Wessex the see of Sherborne was transferred to Old Sarum, which in its turn was replaced by the new cathedral at Salisbury in the thirteenth century.

St Germanus' Church, St German's, Cornwall. Perhaps the most readily recognizable symbol of European Romanesque architecture is the doorway. St Germanus' Church, of monastic origin, has a splendid Norman west doorway, its recessed orders displaying chevron and other typical mouldings. The elliptical form of the arch appears to be the original design, not the result of later settlement.

During the Norman period and throughout the Middle Ages there were four basic types of church, or five if we include private chapels. When visiting a church and trying to work out its history the first thing we should try to discover is which type it is, or was when it was first built. First, there were the secular cathedrals. These were the mother churches of the dioceses, and the seat (or 'cathedra') of the bishop. Under the bishop the cathedral was staffed by a dean and canons. These were secular clergy, not monks, and they lived near the cathedral in individual houses, of which examples survive in the Vicars' Close at Wells, Somerset, and the less complete example at Chichester. The plans of these cathedral churches were derived from the basilican plan we have already noted, but in place of the shallow apsidal sanctuary they had a longer choir, used by the canons when singing the daily services. The nave was used for processions, and for certain services attended by lay people, and the two parts were separated by a substantial stone screen, generally under a central tower. Transepts provided space for additional chapels and altars.

Next, there were the religious houses, abbeys, priories and convents. These were under the rule of an abbot or abbess in the case of the larger establishments, and a prior or prioress for the smaller ones, having the oversight of the monks of nuns. These people lived a communal life, requiring a number of domestic buildings, usually grouped round a cloister or open courtyard on the south side of the church. Incidentally, some of the secular cathedrals also have cloisters, probably copied from monastic examples. The plans of the monastic churches were generally similar to those of the cathedrals.

Then, there were the collegiate churches. Like the secular cathedrals they were generally staffed by a dean and canons, but they were not the seats of bishops. In plan they were similar to the cathedrals and abbeys, though sometimes on a smaller scale, and having the same clear division between the nave and the choir. The choir was used by canons for the services, and the nave for processions and for services to which lay people were admitted. The laity, though, had no rights in the building and no responsibility for its upkeep, and they would, in effect, be regarded as visitors. Some monastic establishments also allowed the laity to use the nave for certain services, but in others they were strictly excluded.

Lastly, there were the parish churches, numerically by far the largest group. These served the local community in town or village, and were

Romsey Abbey Church, Hants. This view of one of the transepts illustrates the massive character of Norman architecture. It shows a variety of capital designs, the stilted arch leading into the chapel (to gain more height), and the dominant character of the triforium above the main arcade.

built and owned by the parishioners except, as we have seen, for the chancels, which were the responsibility of the rectors. The rector would be assisted by other clergy if the parish was large and rich enough, and generally by a parish clerk. The lay people, represented by the churchwardens, had considerable rights in these churches, and were responsible for the building and upkeep of the nave.

In distinguishing between these types of church the position is complicated by the fact that some churches fitted into more than one category. A number of cathedrals were also abbeys, generally of the Benedictine Order, which became very strong and influential after the conquest. The bishop was usually also the abbot, and under him, instead of a dean and chapter of secular canons, were a prior and group of monks. Canterbury was an example of this type of foundation. In other cases an abbey church also served as a parish church. When this was the position the nave generally belonged to the parish and was served by its own clergy, although the abbey would exercise some control over the whole building and its use. The two parts were separated by a substantial screen, in front of which stood the parish altar. Occasionally we find another type of plan with two adjacent parallel naves and chancels, one for the monks or nuns and the other for the parish, as at Saint Helen's Church, Bishopsgate, London. Although now these two 'churches' are separated only by an open arcade there would, in medieval times, have been solid screens between them. Not surprisingly, these 'dual' arrangements often led to disputes between the two parties.

In the later Middle Ages some parish churches became collegiate. The founding of a college was a popular act of piety for rich benefactors, and they were sometimes established in existing churches. This often necessitated alterations and enlargements. Such churches generally remained parochial also, the nave becoming the parish church while the chancel might be enlarged to accommodate the college of priests.

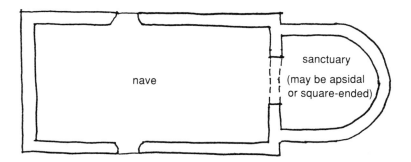

Norman two-cell church plan

Heath Chapel, Shropshire. A unique survival, this small Norman two-cell church stands isolated in fields, having served a now deserted village. Probably for this reason it remains largely unaltered. The ornamented doorway contrasts with the small plain windows. It was probably originally thatched.

Returning now to the Norman parish churches, there were four typical plan forms. First, the two-cell type, consisting of a nave and a chancel. The chancel was sometimes apsidal — a feature reintroduced by the Normans — but this was gradually superseded by the English square-ended chancel. In some very small churches the plan is in fact single-cell, with no structural division between the nave and the chancel.

Next, the three-cell type, with nave, chancel and sanctuary, the latter

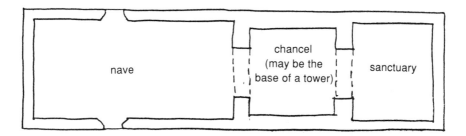

Norman three-cell church plan

37

St Nicholas' Church, Old Shoreham, Sussex, a Norman cruciform church with a central tower. In spite of later windows, and the chapel and vestry added to the north transept, it is the powerful design of the Norman tower which dominates the church.

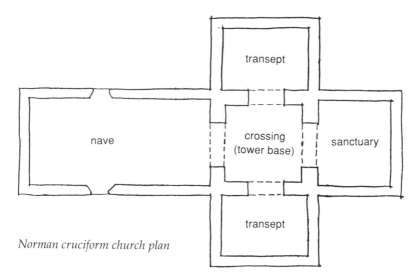

Norman cruciform church plan

being either apsidal or square-ended. Sometimes the chancel formed the base of a central tower.

Next, the cruciform plan, generally with a central tower. The transepts were probably used as side chapels.

LEFT *St James' Church, Coln St Dennis, Glos, a beautiful Norman three-cell church with a central tower, which was raised in the fifteenth century. The chancel windows probably date from the same period as the upper part of the tower, though it is the Norman plan and detailing which give the building its character both inside and out.*

St Lawrence's Church, Pittington, County Durham. The late Norman nave arcade is unusually ornate for a village church. The varied designs of the columns are quite outstanding.

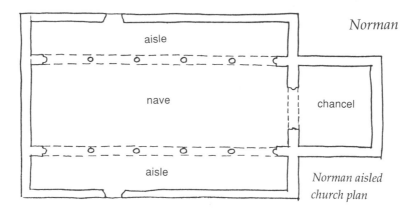

*Norman aisled
church plan*

Lastly, the aisled plan. This was less common in parish churches, except in the largest or wealthiest parishes. More often aisles are found to be an enlargement of an earlier building.

Norman architecture, particularly in its earlier forms, has a massive, rather heavy character, with thick walls compared to those of Saxon buildings, and small round-headed windows, often deeply splayed internally. This was probably due to the influence of the castle builders. Churches were still used as places of refuge in times of danger, and England was in an unsettled state for much of the Norman period. The heavy effect of arches cut through thick walls was sometimes, especially in the later Norman period, lightened by constructing them in a series of recessed stages or 'orders', and enriched by carved mouldings, such as chevron or billet. The chancel arch and the entrance doorway were frequently singled out for particular attention.

The columns in the arcades were generally circular in section, sometimes ornamented by incised spiral or chevron bands. Later in the

St Michael's Church, Garway, Hereford and Worcs. Note the richly ornamented Norman chancel arch of a village church near the Welsh border.

SS Mary and David's Church, Kilpeck, Hereford and Worcs. The carving on the south door of this noted late Norman church shows Scandinavian influence. The detail RIGHT *of one of the jambs depicts a Welsh warrior enmeshed in typical interlacing carving and wearing a Phrygian cap.*

period the heavy effect of a large circular column was reduced by modelling the profile to resemble a series of attached shafts. Capitals were generally of the 'cushion' or scalloped form, but they were sometimes enriched by carving, of grotesque animals, or in a form echoing the classical Corinthian capital.

Norman figure carving is highly stylised showing sometimes Byzantine, sometimes Scandinavian influence. As the external walls were very thick, buttresses were quite shallow and, until later in the period, of little structural significance. The outer wall faces were sometimes decorated with blind arcading, which might be interlaced. Another typical feature of the exterior of Norman churches was the corbel table, a projecting band of stone supporting the eaves of the main roof, or of the tower, itself supported by moulded corbels or carved heads.

These two carvings from St Nicholas' Church, Barfreston, Kent ABOVE and St Mary's Church, Wirksworth, Derbys BELOW show the same subject, Christ in glory, set in a vesica (an oval-shaped frame), surrounded by angels. The sophisticated design of Barfreston, with its arabesque foliage and the intricate figurative detail in the surrounding arches contrasts with the more primitive, but very vigorous work at Wirksworth.

Towers were generally square, very massive, with shallow buttresses and flat or pyramidal roofs. The central tower, popular in Norman times, put a great load on its supporting arches and columns and many of them fell or became unsafe, often to be replaced by a western tower, which became the usual position for the tower in England throughout the Middle Ages. Round towers are sometimes found in districts where good stone, needed to construct strong angles, was not easily available, such as East Anglia and the Sussex downland, both areas where flint was the most common walling material. In these areas stone would have had to be imported for the quoins, arches, columns and similar details, and in areas near the south coast Caen stone was sometimes brought in from Normandy, especially for the larger and wealthier churches. Where good stone was available locally it was used for facing the walls, either as ashlar — smooth cut stone used in regular blocks — or as rougher cut rubble, although the latter, like most flint walling, was generally plastered both inside and out, the stone quoins and other dressings being kept proud of the rubble face to allow for the thickness of the plaster. As mentioned previously, much of this plaster was stripped by Victorian restorers.

In the greater churches, the nave and aisles were constructed as a series of 'bays', a bay being the span between the centres of the arcade columns. The bay consisted of the nave arcade with its arches, the triforium or gallery — a series of arches opening into the space above the aisles — and the clerestory, a range of windows at high level, below the ceiling. In the Norman period the triforium was quite large, but later in the Middle Ages, with the development of vaulting (described later), the height of the clerestory was increased at the expense of that of the triforium, which eventually became simply a shallow band of arcading.

The majority of aisled Norman parish churches were of a simpler form, without a triforium, and did not always have a clerestory, although in later periods the nave roof was sometimes raised to accommodate one, and thus improve the lighting of the nave.

Continuing the Saxon practice, in parishes the rector was usually appointed by the lord of the manor — the successor to the thegn — and this gave the landowner virtual control of the church. In many cases he continued to exercise this right of presentation, but it became increasingly common for it to be given to, or bought by, other patrons. Sometimes the patronage passed to the Crown, either because the lord of the manor fell into disgrace and his estates were confiscated, or because he wanted to ingratiate himself with the king. There are still parishes today where the incumbent is appointed by the Crown, and the origin of this is worth investigating, to throw more light on the history of the church and parish.

Weaverthorpe Church, Yorks. The early Norman tower of this church is unbuttressed, and the absence of windows below belfry level accentuates its austere character. The rest of the church is also Norman, with later inserted windows.

Interlaced arcading, in tiers, at Much Wenlock Abbey, Shropshire; a typical Norman wall treatment, believed by some to be the origin of the pointed arch.

More often, though, the new patrons were the monasteries which thus acquired control over an increasing number of parishes, a process known as impropriation. Sometimes the abbot would appoint a rector in the old way, but often he took the title himself, thus gaining the right to the tithes — a useful addition to the monastic income — and appointed one of his monks or another priest as vicar, or deputy, paid just enough to live on. With rich parishes this process provided increased wealth for the monasteries and did not always increase their popularity. In some cases, though, the patrons carried out their responsibilities and rebuilt the chancels of their churches on a grand scale. The change from lay to religious patronage was not always for the worse.

Apart from this situation, it also became common for other rectors to appoint vicars, or curates, to carry out their work, while they continued to draw the tithes. In some cases one man might be the rector of several parishes, residing in none of them. The Church authorities fought a continuous battle with this custom of pluralities throughout the medieval period and in later centuries. It will generally be found that if an old parish church has a vicar, rather than a rector, this indicates that the patronage was once in the hands of a monastery.

Looking at the internal arrangement of Norman parish churches, there were, apart from architectural details, few changes from Saxon times. There was still no seating in the nave, and little in the chancel. Windows were more often glazed, and stained glass was beginning to appear in the richer churches. The windows, though, were still small, because of the high cost of glass, and some were still being constructed with shutters only.

St Nicholas' Church, Compton, Surrey. This late Norman church has a most unusual feature — a two-storeyed chancel. The lower part is vaulted, and has a segmental chancel arch, while the upper part, probably a chapel, retains its original wooden balustrade.

47

St Mary's Church, Honeychurch, Devon. An attractive small Norman church, altered in the fifteenth century, it retains its original font, with chevron and cable ornament. The cover is Jacobean.

Fonts were still sometimes tub-shaped, but another popular form consisted of a square bowl carried on a thick central column, which might have smaller shafts at the angles. All fonts had to be provided with locked covers, as the baptismal water was blessed at Easter and kept for the whole year, and there was a fear that it might be stolen for purposes of witchcraft. The internal walls of the church were usually decorated with paintings, sometimes in patterns to imitate jointed stonework, or simple floral designs. Often, though, pictorial subjects were chosen, scenes from the Bible or the lives of the saints, designed for teaching at a time when religious books were nearly all in Latin and few lay people could read. In the church at Halling, Kent, where the patron was the Cathedral Abbey of Rochester, there is, near the chancel arch, a wall painting of the Last Supper showing the Apostles dressed as Benedictine monks!

48

ABOVE *Norman wall paintings on the barrel-vaulted roof of the chancel of St Mary's Church, Kempley, Glos. The figure of Christ in glory can be seen in the centre.*

RIGHT *The painting of the Last Supper above the chancel arch at Halling Church, Kent shows the Apostles dressed as Benedictine monks.*

St Mary's Church, Stow, Lincs. The evolution from Norman to Gothic architecture is shown in this fine church by the ribbed vaults in the chancel, and the use of the pointed arch, with its additional strength, to support the weight of the central tower.

4

From Norman to Gothic

It is generally agreed that the evolution of the Gothic style of architecture from the Romanesque began in northern France, and what is probably the earliest example of Transitional Gothic in England, the choir of Canterbury Cathedral, was designed by a French master mason. Various theories have been put forward for the evolution of the use of the pointed arch, the main distinguishing mark of Gothic architecture. Some think it was brought back to Europe by the crusaders who had seen pointed arches in Saracenic buildings; others that it developed from the common Romanesque pattern of interlaced arcading as wall decoration. It is most likely, though, that the advantages of the pointed arch were first appreciated in connection with stone vaulting, and that from this beginning its structural superiority over the round arch made possible the later developments of the Gothic style.

Most of the Norman churches were originally roofed with timber, covered with thatch or shingles, although lead was sometimes used on the more important buildings. The risk of fire was always present, and the aim of the builders of churches, castles and important houses was to protect their work with a fire-proof roof; that is, a stone vault. In some Norman churches we find the chancel vaulted while the nave is roofed in timber.

Vaulting had been used by the Romans, in concrete, and the Normans had inherited some of their methods, using a coarse type of concrete of small stones or rubble, set in mortar, cast on wooden shuttering and afterwards plastered. The simplest form of vault was the semi-circular tunnel, or barrel vault. Above this was constructed a timber roof finished with thatch, shingles or lead. The weight of this outer roof and that of the vault itself exerted an outward thrust, as well as a direct load, on the side walls of the building, producing a tendency for them to spread, and as this thrust was distributed equally along the walls they had to be very thick, and openings kept to a minimum, to withstand it.

The first refinement of this technique was the introduction of the cross,

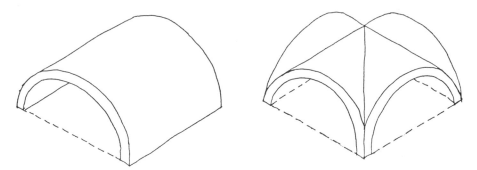

Early vaults. LEFT *A tunnel or barrel vault;* RIGHT *a cross or groined vault, both of solid construction.*

or groined vault. Here, in addition to the main longitudinal tunnel, there were several transverse tunnels intersecting it at right angles, producing, as one looks up, a series of squares with diagonals, the whole vault being constructed as before in rubble concrete. This had two advantages. First, windows could be placed higher up in the walls, in the centres of the

LEFT *St Michael's Church, Ewenny, Mid-Glamorgan, Wales. Here, the nave has a barrel vault, with cross-ribs, while the chancel has a groined vault, ribbed, allowing for a higher level window.* ABOVE *Early groined vaults, with cross-ribs, at SS Mary and Martin's Priory Church, Blyth, Notts.*

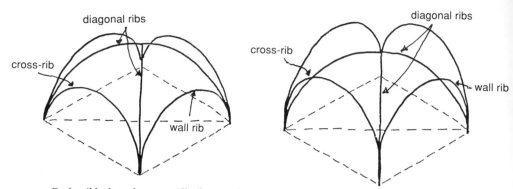

*Early ribbed vaults:*LEFT *All ribs round-arched. The diagonal ribs rise above the cross-ribs, producing an uneven ridge line.* RIGHT *Here the cross and wall ribs are stilted (raised on short vertical sections) to produce a level ridge line. Infillings are not shown.*

arches, and second, the outward thrust of the vault, instead of being distributed equally along the wall, was concentrated at regular points, where it could be met by buttresses, allowing the rest of the wall to be thinner and windows to be larger.

These solid cross-vaults were still very heavy, and expensive and difficult to construct, because of the elaborate shuttering or temporary wooden support needed to carry them until the mortar had set. They were generally confined to small areas such as chancels, porches and aisles; the means of resisting the thrust from a vault over a high nave, in an aisled church, had not yet been discovered. A new system was therefore developed in which arches, following the lines of the groins (the intersections between the vault surfaces) and of the junctions of the vault with the outer walls, were first built up, using cut stone, and then a lighter infilling laid between them. These ribbed vaults required only a light wooden 'centre' to support the arches (or ribs) while they were being built, and these centres could be re-used as the work proceeded. These ribbed vaults were first used in England in Durham Cathedral in about AD1100.

A difficulty had arisen though, in building the arched ribs. A semi-circular arch rising from the diagonal of a square will be higher than those rising from the sides of the square, and this will produce a vault of varying height. This could be overcome either by making the diagonal ribs *elliptical* (as the groins in a solid cross-vault had been) or by raising the wall and cross ribs on stilts. These latter look rather clumsy, while an elliptical arch is structurally rather weak. The masons eventually solved their problem by using pointed arches which, by adjusting the centres from which the curves are struck, can produce arches of almost any height from a given span. To start with, pointed arches were used for the wall and cross ribs, retaining semi-circular arches for the diagonal ribs, but the realisation of the greater strength of the pointed arch led to its

ABOVE *In Beverley Minster, Humberside, pointed arches are used for the cross-ribs, retaining round arches for the diagonal ribs.*

Later rib vaults: LEFT *Pointed arches are used for the cross and wall ribs to raise them level with the diagonal ribs.* RIGHT *A similar vault, but with the addition of ridge ribs to achieve greater rigidity in the structure.*

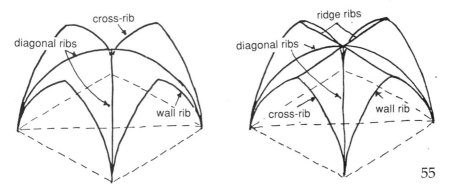

55

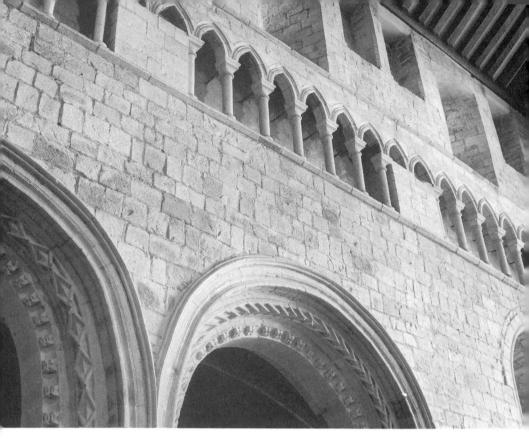

St Mary's Church, Cartmel, Cumbria. This former priory church was built in the late twelfth century, and shows the transition from Norman to Gothic architecture. The arches of the nave arcade are round, but the mouldings are more refined than those of true Norman work. The arches of the triforium are pointed, but rise from Norman cushion capitals.

general use in vaulting. When the nave of Chichester Cathedral was re-roofed after a fire in AD1187 a ribbed vault of this form was used. Later, longitudinal ribs were introduced along the ridge (the highest point of the vault) to provide extra stability. The intersections of the ribs were generally marked by stone bosses, providing scope for carved decoration.

Once the Norman builders had discovered the usefulness of the pointed arch in vaulting they went on to exploit it throughout their buildings, and its greater strength and opportunities for more flexible design led to the evolution of early Gothic architecture. For a time the two arch forms continued side by side, and round and pointed arches were used in the same building. We may find pointed arches retaining Norman mouldings and ornament, and round arches where the mouldings have the more refined character of early Gothic work. Eventually, though, the use of the pointed arch predominated, and the round arch almost disappeared from English architecture until the Renaissance.

St Margaret's Church, Kings Lynn, Norfolk. The wall arcading shows the transition from Norman to Gothic. The bottom stage has interlaced round arches, while the upper stage has pointed trefoiled arches, all probably contemporary.

5

Early Gothic

In the last chapter we saw how the Gothic style of architecture evolved from the Romanesque as an answer to the problem of vaulting a large roof, and how, once the builders had appreciated the structural potential of the pointed arch, they went on to exploit it. This brought about the first real change in architectural style for many centuries. Until about the middle of the twelfth century the Romanesque style in western Europe, like the Byzantine style in the East, had been greatly influenced by Roman architecture, and few new structural developments had taken place.

Now, though, a completely new style of architecture was being created which was to continue to develop for the next three centuries, and which in England at least was never completely forgotten, re-appearing at intervals and in isolated places throughout the seventeenth and eighteenth centuries, when classical influence was dominant. The early Gothic style, developed as we have seen, to solve the problems of vaulting the great cathedrals, was soon to influence the design of even the humblest parish churches.

The chief characteristics of the new style were a growing lightness and refinement, moving away from the massive nature of Norman work, and with a greater emphasis on the vertical line. The circular columns of the nave arcades were now more slender, and were often surrounded by separate shafts, sometimes of a different stone, such as polished Purbeck Marble (in fact, a hard limestone, not a true marble). The capitals to columns were either moulded, the mouldings being bolder and more deeply cut than those of the Norman period, or were enriched with stiff-leaf carving, under a flat circular slab, or abacus.

All mouldings were now more deeply defined, even at times undercut, and the most characteristic ornament was the dog-tooth, perhaps derived from the Norman nail-head. External walls were still decorated with blind

St Mary's Church, Westwell, Kent. This fine thirteenth-century village church has a triple chancel arch, with circular columns and trefoiled arches — an echo perhaps of the much earlier basilican plan.

59

St Andrew's Church, Chedworth, Glos. Typical thirteenth-century stiff-leaf foliage on the capitals of the chancel arch, under half-octagonal abaci.

arcading, but this was often more deeply recessed than before, sometimes forming a series of niches filled with statues, particularly on the west fronts of cathedral and abbey churches. Sculpture was playing an increasingly important part in the decoration of churches, and the west fronts of the greater churches came to be treated as screens for the display of figure sculpture, one of the finest examples of the period being that at Wells Cathedral, Somerset.

External walls were now thinner, with the thrust from the roof being taken by buttresses, which were given greater projection. Flying buttresses — half-arches carried above the aisle roofs — were designed to solve the problem of meeting the thrust from the high vaults of the nave. Towers were now more slender than in Norman times and were given spires, perhaps a development of the Norman pyramid tower roofs. At this period, the broach spire was the most common form. In this design, the octagonal spire was, in effect, mitred on to the square base, the whole overhanging the tower slightly and corbelled out from it. The defensive aspect of tower design was now becoming less important; the tower was designed to contain bells, and increasingly as an architectural feature — even a status symbol as, throughout the Middle Ages, parishes seemed to vie with each other to build the finest and tallest towers.

Church roofs were generally steeply pitched, covered with thatch or shingles on the smaller churches, and lead on the larger and richer ones. In spite of the developments in vaulting described in the last chapter, most parish churches still had timber roofs. Comparatively few roofs of

St Michael's Church, Chesterton, Cambs. The church is mainly of the thirteenth century and has a typical broach spire. The porch and aisle windows are eighteenth-century work.

61

St Mary's Church, West Walton, Norfolk. The whole church is of the thirteenth century. The tower, with its ranges of blind arcading and huge plate-traceried belfry windows, was built detached from the church, probably because of marshy ground, as a safeguard against the risk of differential subsidence.

this early Gothic period have survived, but they were generally of the simple trussed rafter form, with tie-beams at intervals to check the thrust on the walls.

Great developments were taking place in window design. The small round-headed Norman windows gave way to rather larger lancets, tall windows with pointed-arched heads and sometimes deeply splayed reveals, further enriched with an inner or rere-arch supported on small shafts or columns. The next development was to group two or more lancets together, giving the effect of a larger window. Sometimes a circular window was inserted above the lancets, and all enclosed in an outer arch, forming what is known as 'plate tracery'. From this was developed 'bar tracery'; that is, the dividing up of a large window into several vertical divisions of 'lights' (derived from the original lancets), by moulded stone uprights or mullions, with tracery of a geometrical design filling the space between the heads of the lights and the main outer arch. The heads of the lights, and the tracery shapes, would be ornamented with curved projections or 'cusps' to produce trefoil or cinquefoil arches.

The chancel at Bottesford Church, Lincs, has lancet windows of exceptionally narrow and tall proportions. In the transept wall are a circular window and two lancets. When close together, these form the units of plate tracery.

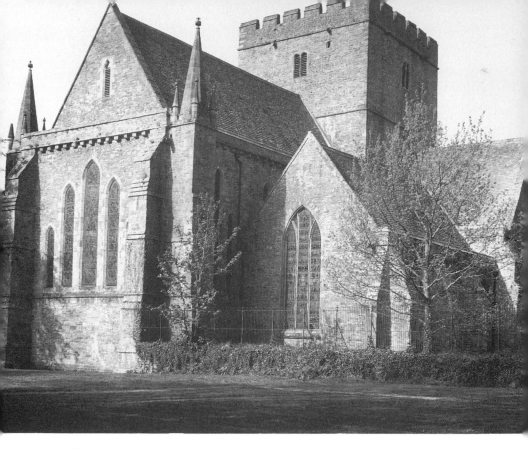

Brecon Cathedral, Powys, Wales. The east window consists of five stepped lancets, a typical thirteenth-century form. Note the corbel table above the window — a survival of Norman design.

This evolution of tracery design in windows, and increase in window areas, was paralleled by the development of stained glass, which became one of the major church arts. Most of the glass of this early period is richly coloured, except for the light 'grisaille' patterned glass, seen at its best in the Five Sisters window in York Minster. The most usual form of early thirteenth-century glass was, though, a series of richly coloured medallions, illustrating scenes from the Bible and lives of the saints. Like the wall paintings these windows were designed primarily as visual aids for a still largely illiterate people.

Porches were often added to parish churches at this period, to provide protection from the weather and to help keep the church interior free from draughts. Churches still had little or no heating. Also, certain parts of the services would be held in the porch; for instance, the first part of the marriage service. Some porches had upper rooms, used either as living accommodation for a priest, for storage, or as a schoolroom. In areas where building stone was scarce porches were sometimes built of timber.

In the greater churches, the bay design shows a reduction in the size of the triforium and a corresponding increase in that of the clerestory, this being made easier by the use of vaulting instead of a flat ceiling. There was also a general lightening of the structure, compared with Norman work. To meet the needs of a growing population and an increase in prosperity, many parish churches were enlarged at this period by building aisles, which sometimes incorporated, and largely obliterated, the transepts of an original cruciform church. A north aisle was more often added first since, as we have seen, this side of the churchyard was less likely to be encumbered by burials. The most significant feature of thirteenth-century church development was, though, the need to build

St Cross Hospital, Winchester, Hants. A thirteenth century doorway with plate tracery, and trefoil-headed arches, very similar in form to the typical plate tracery window.

Holy Cross Abbey Church, Pershore, Hereford and Worcs. The surviving chancel of the church has clustered columns with stiff-leaf capitals and deeply moulded arches. The rere-arches of the clerestory windows are carried down to mask the triforium.

66

larger chancels to accommodate the more elaborate ceremonial now being developed. Although small two-cell churches were still being built in small country parishes, many Norman churches had their short chancels rebuilt at this time, and the square east end was by now almost universal in England. Similarly in the greater churches, the cathedrals and abbeys, the choirs were often rebuilt on a larger scale and the monks or canons seated in these new eastern extensions, rather than under the crossing tower, which had been the more usual Norman practice.

Another feature of the period was a growing devotion to the saints, particularly to the Virgin Mary, Our Lady. Many Lady Chapels were added to churches at this time. In the greater churches these were generally at the east end, beyond the choir, resulting in a further eastward extension of the church. In parish churches they are more usually found as aisles to the chancel or nave. It now became common for even the smallest churches to have several altars, dedicated to popular saints and often endowed by private benefactors or by the religious or trade guilds. Today, the only evidence of many of these former altars is the existence of a piscina, an arched recess in the wall containing a drain, where the communion vessels were washed. This always indicates the position of an altar.

Fixed seating was now occasionally found in the naves of churches, generally in the form of stone benches around the walls, and sometimes round the column bases. These were intended mainly for the old and infirm, and are believed to be the origin of the phrase 'the weakest to the wall'. The floors of the smaller churches were probably still of beaten earth, but this was beginning to be superseded by stone or tiled paving. Decorative, encaustic tiles were laid in the greater churches and the richer parish churches, and these can still sometimes be found, particularly in the chancel.

The fonts of this period were generally smaller than the Norman ones, but still large enough to allow for total immersion in infant baptism. Monuments were now more common in churches, but only for the richer and more important parishioners, who were buried in the church rather than in the churchyard. Sculptured effigies (not necessarily actual portraits at this time) were most common, but towards the end of the thirteenth century monumental brasses appeared. In many cases, though, the actual brasses have disappeared, leaving only the recess in the surrounding stone known as the matrix. All these monuments provide valuable evidence for the costume of the period.

Wall paintings were still carried out, and where they survive give us a good impression of the appearance of early Gothic churches. With our rather more restrained tastes, we would probably find them quite garish

All Saints' Church, Sutton Bingham, Somerset. Wall paintings of c.1300, showing the Coronation of the Virgin. The uncovering and repair of medieval wall paintings has been a feature of the restoration work of recent years.

and overpowering in character in their original condition and extent. The sculpture of this period was vigorous in nature, and often shows a sense of humour, and a lack of distinction between the sacred and the secular that perhaps we find hard to understand. As we shall see in a later chapter, the Victorians had an idealistic and refined view of the early Middle Ages which was in many ways far from the truth.

This early Gothic style was one of continuous growth and development. It is difficult to say exactly when it evolved from the Norman style, but it was fully developed by the early thirteenth century. By the end of the century it was already changing in character, but this was a more gradual evolution, unlike the great changes resulting from the discovery of the possibilities of the pointed arch.

St Helen's Church, Cliffe-at-Hoo, Kent. Thirteenth-century wall paintings in the transept, with trefoiled arches framing the pictorial scenes from lives of the saints. The Victorian passion for bare stone has resulted in the loss of original painting from the jamb stones of the window.

69

6

Later Gothic

At the end of the last chapter I suggested that there is no real hard and fast dividing line between the Early English Gothic style and the Decorated style which succeeded it. We should remember that these names, commonly used today, of Early English, Decorated and Perpendicular to describe the three styles of English Gothic architecture, were not used in their own day but were coined in the last century, probably by Thomas Rickman, an architect, at a time when interest in medieval architecture was first being taken seriously. Other sequences suggested at that time, but which failed to gain general popularity were First, Second and Third Pointed, and Lancet, Geometrical, Curvilinear and Rectilinear, these last being based on the development of window tracery. In some ways these style names are rather misleading, particularly when definite date limits are set to them. People did not stop building in one style and start in another during any one year. There have, of course, been some definite landmarks in English church design: the Norman conquest of 1066; the construction of the ribbed vaults over the nave of Durham Cathedral c.1100; the rebuilding of Canterbury Cathedral choir, starting in 1175; but once the Gothic style had been evolved it continued to do so gradually, at least until the middle of the fourteenth century when, as we shall see, there was another definite change. The Decorated style, though, evolved continuously from the Early English, from the late thirteenth century onwards. The main features of this new development were as follows.

Vaulting became more elaborate, with the insertion of intermediate, or 'tierceron' ribs, between the main ribs, thus reducing the area to be spanned between them and producing a richer effect. This can be well seen in the nave of Exeter Cathedral, and the retro-choir of Wells Cathedral. Later on, 'lierne', or connecting ribs were introduced, spanning

St Clements' Church, Terrington St Clement, Norfolk, one of the great marshland churches, largely rebuilt in the fifteenth century. The window tracery, and the panelling to the parapets and the porch, are typical of this period.

between the main and the tierceron ribs, producing a star-like pattern. As the number of ribs increased, so did their intersections and the numbers of bosses, providing the medieval stone carver with great opportunities for ornament and inventiveness. These bosses are always worth studying, even if this involves some discomfort in looking straight upwards.

Window tracery developed from the early geometrical forms described in the last chapter, becoming more richly cusped, and sometimes producing a reticulated, or net-like pattern. From this stage the tracery evolved into a flowing, or curvilinear pattern, featuring the double curve, or ogee line. Hand in hand with this development went that of stained

BELOW LEFT *The fourteenth-century east window, with reticulated tracery, of Bainton Church, Humberside.* BELOW RIGHT *St John the Baptist's Church, Shottesbrooke, Berks is a complete fourteenth-century church, with an octagonal spire rising from behind a parapet, and a fine curvilinear traceried east window.*

LEFT *The lierne vault to the east end of Tewkesbury Abbey, Glos.*

glass, which became lighter in tone. The old, deeply coloured medallions, typical of the thirteenth century, gave way to larger single figures under canopies. The Tree of Jesse was a favourite subject in the large east windows. Although the pointed arch was used for most openings the square-headed window is also found in work of the early fourteenth century. As we shall see, it was to reappear at the end of the Middle Ages.

Buttresses became still bolder in their projection, as the walls became thinner, and the windows larger. Diagonally set angle-buttresses were now common on towers, and at other external angles.

In the planning of churches, further provision was made for additional altars, generally in side chapels, although altars were also sometimes sited on each side of the central opening in the chancel screen. The religious and trade guilds were growing in importance, especially in the towns, and often had their own chapels in the parish church, served by their own chaplains. Aisles were added, rebuilt or widened to accommodate extra altars and a growing population. The chancel arches of this period were generally wider than earlier ones, and older chancel arches were sometimes widened at this time. The tendency to open up the interior of the church increased, although the chancel and chapels were always screened off from the nave.

Because of the influence of the friars, who had reached England from the continent in the fourteenth century, preaching was now becoming more important. Pulpits were first introduced into parish churches at this time, although they were still comparatively rare. Bench seats began to appear in the naves of churches, the earliest of these being very plain, often backless, like forms. Timber roofs were becoming more elaborate. Tie-beam and king-post roofs appeared, as did arch-braced collar and tie-beam roofs. In roofs of these types the weight of the common rafters was transferred to longitudinal members or purlins, supported on the main trusses, rather than every pair of rafters being trussed, as in the earlier roofs. In some areas, though, particularly in the east of England, the trussed rafter and crown-post roof continued in use. However, in spite of these developments in roof design, carved ornament tended to be concentrated on stonework rather than on woodwork.

The internal walls were still decorated with paintings, although as window areas became larger, stained glass was becoming the more important teaching medium. Both foliage and figure sculpture were now more naturalistic. The ball-flower ornament replaced the dog-tooth, and the ogee curve was used in arches, particularly over smaller openings where its structural weakness, compared with that of the pointed arch, was less important.

This Decorated style of the late thirteenth and early fourteenth centuries

St Helen's Church, Leverton, Lincs. The sedilia, with crocketed ogee-arched canopies, vaulted on the underside.

was exuberant and lively, but it was comparatively short-lived. By the middle of the fourteenth century a considerable change was coming over English church architecture. This change is sometimes attributed to the effects of the Black Death, that outbreak of bubonic plague which reached England in 1348 and spread across the country with devastating effect, greatly reducing the population and bringing some drastic economic and social changes. In fact, though, the evolution of the new Perpendicular style, found only in England, had begun before the plague arrived. Various theories have been put forward about the origins of this style of architecture. The earliest surviving example is probably the choir of Gloucester Abbey (now the Cathedral), built in 1337, but earlier evidence of the new style was seen in Saint Stephen's Chapel, Westminster, and in the chapter house of Old Saint Paul's Cathedral, London, in 1332. These latter buildings (both now destroyed) were the work of the Court masons, who may also have influenced the work at Gloucester. This reconstruction of Gloucester choir was made possible by the large income the monks gained from pilgrims visiting the tomb of the murdered King Edward II, itself a fine example of the *Decorated* style. It is perhaps significant, though, that the Norman choir at Gloucester was not demolished and

ABOVE *SS Peter and Paul's Church, Lavenham, Suffolk. The four-centred arched windows with Perpendicular tracery, and the enriched parapets and buttresses, are typical features.* ABOVE RIGHT *The fifteenth-century north aisle of St Michael's Church, Stinsford, Dorset, with square-headed Perpendicular windows.*

rebuilt, but simply cased and remodelled in the new style. Similar remodellings were later carried out to the naves of Winchester Cathedral, and Sherborne Abbey, Dorset, suggesting perhaps that the Church no longer had such great funds available for complete rebuilding.

The main characteristic of the Perpendicular style was the replacement of the flowing, naturalistic lines of the Decorated style by predominantly vertical lines, crossed by horizontals, producing something of a gridiron effect in window tracery and wall panelling. The tracery was thus simplified, although the windows were often larger than ever before, forming a frame for stained glass. This peculiarly English development of the Gothic style was in complete contrast to what happened in France and other European countries, where the Decorated style evolved into the Flamboyant, with even more flowing and sinuous lines, particularly in window tracery.

Arches were generally wider than in the previous periods, and by the fifteenth century the four-centred (sometimes known as the 'Tudor') arch was becoming popular. Square-headed windows are occasionally found,

particularly later in the period, distinguished from those of the Decorated style by their different tracery. Later in the fifteenth century, in doorways, the four-centred arch would be enclosed in a rectangular frame, the resultant spandrils — the spaces between the outside of the arch and the frame — providing opportunity for carved ornament, frequently heraldic in character.

Mouldings were generally simpler and shallower than in earlier periods, but were often enriched with carving. Foliage carving was again less naturalistic and more formal in character, but much flatter in appearance than that of the early thirteenth century. Arcade columns

St Patrick's Church, Patrington, Humberside. The fourteenth-century capitals have foliage carving, but it is much flatter in character than that of the thirteenth century. Compare with the illustration on page 60.

St Nicholas' Church, Kings Lynn, Norfolk. The lierne vault to the porch.

were now octagonal, sometimes with slightly hollowed faces and octagonal moulded capitals. Clustered columns are also found, with moulded or carved capitals, but sometimes the mouldings of the arch ran directly into those of the columns, without capitals.

Vaulting became even more elaborate than before, with the introduction of more lierne ribs, enhancing the star-like effect. The panels between the ribs often now consisted of single pieces of stone, this being known as 'rib and panel' vaulting. Still further opportunities were thus provided for elaborately carved bosses. The ultimate development was the fan vault, in which separate ribs and panels were replaced by cones formed of solid stone, with the ribs simply worked on the surface. These fan vaults produced practically no outward thrust on the walls, allowing them to consist of large windows separated by buttresses. A further elaboration was pendant fan vaulting, the vaults in this case being hung from stone transverse arches, of which the pendants were enlarged voussoirs (wedge-shaped arch-stones). The best known example of this is at King Henry VII's Chapel, Westminster Abbey. In many of the greater churches built at this time the triforium had disappeared, and the tracery of the clerestory windows was continued downwards as panelling to the walling above the arcade.

LEFT *St Mary's Church, Saffron Waldon, Essex, a fine late fifteenth-century church. Note the paired clerestory windows, their mullions continued downwards to form wall panelling, and the traceried panelled spandrils to the arches of the nave arcade.*

79

St Andrew's Church, Cullompton, Devon. The fan vault in the Lane aisle. Because it was built at the request of a specific benefactor, it can be firmly dated to 1525.

This new style was in some ways simpler than its predecessor, at least as far as masonry was concerned. It was more regular and mechanical in design and could be carried out by less skilled craftsmen, and after the Black Death had wiped out about a third of the population of England there must have been a shortage of craftsmen. This factor may have helped the new style to become established, and it continued to flourish until the mid-sixteenth century — a longer period than that of the whole of the two earlier Gothic styles.

Many villages were depopulated as a result of the outbreaks of plague and the consequent economic changes, and, in contrast to the earlier phases of church enlargement, we sometimes find, in the mid to late fourteenth century, evidence of churches having been reduced in size by the demolition of aisles and building up of the arcades. Other churches were allowed to become ruinous or were turned into barns, their congregations never recovering. By the fifteenth century, though, the population had started to increase again, and there was a great new programme of parish church building, especially in areas such as East Anglia and parts of the West country, where the growth of the wool and cloth trades brought a period of new prosperity. Many churches were completely rebuilt in this period, and others were greatly enlarged.

There seems to have been at this time a great pre-occupation with the thought of death — not perhaps surprising after the disasters of the plague. It was at this period that many chantries were founded, both by private individuals and by the religious and trade guilds. A chantry was an endowment to pay a priest to say prayers and masses for the soul of the founder. Sometimes it was founded at an existing altar in the church, but often a separate chapel was built, being either added to the building or screened off in an aisle. Some chantry chapels were completely enclosed structures — a church within a church. Many of them are very

A chantry chapel in Tewkesbury Abbey, Glos, vaulted and ornamented, and with some heraldic motifs — a church within a church. After the Black Death, prayers for the dead assumed a greater significance in the medieval Church.

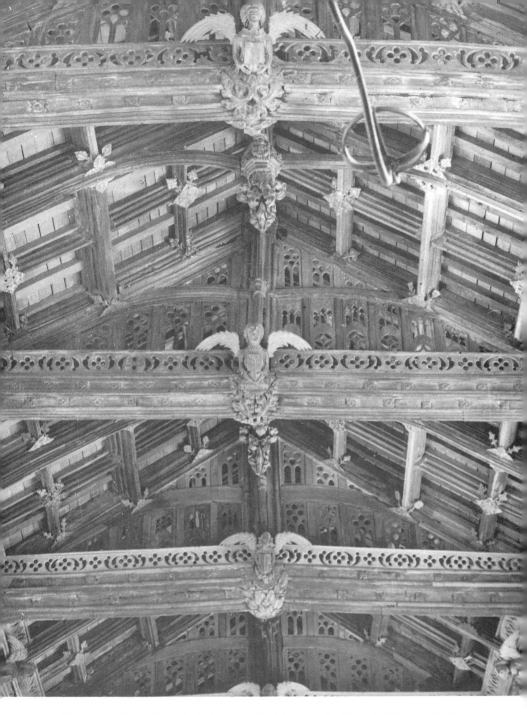

The ornate low-pitched tie-beam roof of St Mary's Church, Weston Zoyland, Somerset. Note that the tie-beams, each made from a single timber, are not straight, but slightly cambered for strength.

82

Detail of the double hammer-beam roof, with its angel carvings, at Knapton, Norfolk.

beautiful, containing fine sculptures and paintings. They usually contained the tombs of the donor and his family, and a tendency developed for the family to sit in its own chapel for the Sunday Mass. In town parishes, where a number of chantries had been founded, the chantry priests sometimes lived a communal life, in their own building, known as a college.

While, as we have seen, masonry tended to become more stereotyped in design during the Perpendicular period, carpentry developed as never before, and the carpenter came into his own. This was the great age of timber roof construction. In place of the simple trussed rafter roofs we find far more elaborate arch-braced tie and collar-beam roofs, now flatter in pitch as lead roofing became more common, rather than thatch or shingle. Where trussed rafter roofs were still used they were sometimes panelled internally in timber or plaster, with decorative ribs and bosses, a form particularly popular in parts of the West Country and known as a waggon or barrel roof. As a final development we find the hammer-beam roof, seen at its best in East Anglian churches, often coloured and gilded, and enriched with carved angels. It was usual for the roof above the rood

ABOVE *St James' Church, Swimbridge, Devon. Detail of the vaulting to the rood screen, a typical West Country feature.* RIGHT *The rood screen of All Saints' Church, Theddlethorpe, Lincs. The absence of vaulting (rarely found in eastern counties) and the removal of the loft have left the screen with rather a truncated appearance.*

loft to be more richly decorated than that over the rest of the nave, and the roof over the altar would also be given special treatment.

The screens also reached their finest development at this time, particularly in the West Country, with timber vaulting supporting the loft. By this time it was becoming usual for the loft to be occupied by singers, and sometimes a small organ. Church music was more elaborate, especially in the larger and richer churches, with the early plainsong replaced by counterpoint or harmony. By the fifteenth century fixed seating was more usual in churches, and the bench ends provided more opportunities for the wood carver. There was still, though, plenty of space left between the blocks of seating. Churches were not crowded with pews as some have become today. For some time seating had been provided in the choirs of the greater churches, for the monks or canons. The tip-up seats are known as misericords, and fine carvings, which may be completely secular in character, are found under them.

Font covers, particularly in East Anglia, developed into miniature steeples, and the fonts themselves, generally now octagonal in plan, were often enriched with carving, the Seven Sacraments being a favourite theme. The font bowls were generally smaller than in previous periods.

84

Pulpits were becoming more common, reflecting the growing importance of preaching — perhaps foreshadowing the changes that were soon to come. Monumental sculpture was of a very high standard, and many examples survive from this period.

St Mary's Church, Swine, Humberside. Alabaster table-tombs. The shields on the side would originally have borne painted coats of arms of the deceased.

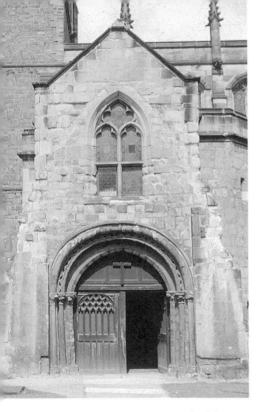

ABOVE *The Norman porch of St Mary's Church, Shrewsbury, Shropshire, was given an upper storey in the fifteenth century.* RIGHT *The fifteenth-century timber-framed porch of St James' Church, Stanstead Abbots, Herts.*

In plan, the parish churches were really developing into pillared halls, with no structural division between the nave and the chancel. Such churches sometimes look rather bare to us today, but we must remember that they were originally divided up with screens and far more brightly coloured than most of them are now. Porches, sometimes two-storeyed, could be richly decorated, and additional storeys were sometimes added to earlier porches to provide a room for a priest, or a schoolroom. Church towers were finer than ever, although spires were less common, the tower being more often finished with an ornamental parapet. It seems that in some areas parishes were vying with one another to construct the finest tower.

St Mary's Church, Huish Episcopi, Somerset, the fine fifteenth-century west tower, one of a host of fine church towers typical of this part of Somerset. The niches would originally have held statues.

Stained glass was becoming more naturalistic in treatment, and the glass in a church now tended to follow a definite theme around the church, telling the story of the Bible pictorially from the Creation to the Last Judgement. So much medieval glass has been destroyed that it is difficult for us to visualise this, but at Fairford, Gloucestershire, and King's College Chapel, Cambridge, the glass survives intact and its theme can be studied.

Lychgates usually date from the fourteenth century and later. They were built at the entrance to the churchyard to shelter the coffin (or 'lych') while the first part of the burial service was held here. Some of these early lychgates have a raised platform on which the coffin could be rested.

By the end of the fifteenth century, in spite of the disturbances of the Wars of the Roses, English church architecture had probably reached its peak. Even in small and humble parishes the churches were richly decorated and furnished, as is shown by the Inventories of King Edward VI's Commissioners (to which we shall refer later). Very few churches remain today in anything like their condition at that time, but a few fortunate survivors can give us some idea of what they must all have been like. Parish church building was then more often financed by wealthy merchants than by the lord of the manor, since the Wars of the Roses had weakened the position and status of the old aristocracy. Funds were also raised by the parishioners, often by means of the church ales, which combined money-raising with social activities. The old inns sometimes found adjoining the churchyard, with signs of a religious origin, probably occupy the sites of the alehouses used on these occasions by the churchwardens for brewing the ale. In some parishes church houses were built for these activities — forerunners of the modern church hall.

The late fifteenth and early sixteenth centuries were a great age of parish church building. On the whole less work was being carried out to the cathedrals and abbeys, although the rebuilding of Bath Abbey was still in progress at the time of the Dissolution. By now, though, the chief influence as centres of culture and learning was passing from the abbeys to the colleges and schools, many of which, founded by churchmen, date from this period. One of the most famous buildings of this last phase of Gothic architecture is King's College Chapel, Cambridge, typical of this new emphasis. Its glass, and the woodwork of the screen, show the early influence of the Renaissance, but its architecture is still entirely Gothic, and traditional. In the window jambs can be seen canopied niches, designed to hold statues of the saints, but there is no evidence that such statues were ever fixed there. As is shown by the survival of the glass, this chapel largely escaped damage by the iconoclasts. Carved decoration

The Church House, Crowcombe, Somerset. Given to the Church in 1515, this was used for the brewing and selling of church ales, and other social functions. Later used as an almshouse, it has now been restored to church use.

there is, all around the walls, but this consists of variations of the Royal Coat of Arms. Perhaps this feature, which dates from well before King Henry VIII's matrimonial troubles, indicates the first signs of the great changes which were soon to come, and which will be the subject of the next chapter.

King's College Chapel, Cambridge. The predominance of the Royal Arms and other royal symbols in the decoration of this chapel foreshadows the changes soon to come in the life of the Church and the nation.

7

The Reformation

The Reformation in the mid-sixteenth century was probably the greatest upheaval in the life and history of the Church of England, and it has had many lasting effects on church buildings. These effects were increased by the fact that chronologically the Reformation coincided with the arrival in England of the new ideas of the Renaissance, with its emphasis on Classical study and art forms. Medieval architecture and medieval churchmanship fell out of favour at the same time. Even today, the Reformation and its effects are highly controversial subjects, but in this chapter I shall try to avoid controversy and concentrate on the physical effects of the various phases of the Reformation on our churches.

At the end of the last chapter I described King's College Chapel, Cambridge, where figures of the saints had been superseded by representations of the Royal Arms as subjects for the interior decoration of a church, and pointed out that this work had been carried out while King Henry VIII still acknowledged the authority of the Pope. Whatever our views are on the Reformation I think it is generally accepted that it would probably have happened, to some degree and in some form, even if Henry had not, in his desire for an heir, decided to seek a new wife. It was one manifestation of the growing sense of nationalism which affected England and much of Europe.

In England, the first move in this direction was the king's repudiation of the authority of the Pope over the Church of England, in the Act of Supremacy in 1534. What effect did this have on the Church? First, there was an abrupt end to the building boom in parish churches which had marked the fifteenth and early sixteenth centuries. At a time of great uncertainty about the future of the Church, and growing religious controversy as the influence of the Continental reformers began to be felt, with the pendulum of religious opinion swinging first one way, then the other, it was only to be expected that people would be less interested in spending money on church buildings. For the next hundred years, therefore, comparatively few new churches were built, and in looking at this period we shall be mainly concerned with the alterations carried out to existing churches. Apart from this, though, the replacement of the Pope by the King as head of the Church probably made little difference in most parishes. No changes were made in the church services, or in the general life of the Church, and only a minority of the clergy were deprived of their livings for refusing to accept the Act of Supremacy. It can be revealing to study the lists of rectors or vicars in an old church, and to see how they survived the Reformation changes.

Next, from 1536 to 1539, came the Dissolution of the monasteries, and this certainly resulted in some material changes. How did the monastic churches fare at this time? In a later chapter we shall be looking at the problem of redundant churches today, and how the Church is now approaching it. The Tudors were completely materialistic and ruthless in their attitude to this situation. To start with, we should remember that a number of the cathedrals — including Canterbury, but not York — were also abbeys. Here the prior and the monks were replaced by a dean and chapter of canons — secular clergy. In some cases the last prior became the first dean, and the transition was relatively simple. The domestic monastic buildings, no longer required for the community life, were either demolished or converted into individual houses for the canons, but on the whole the churches remained untouched. The secular cathedrals suffered no real change at this time, and many of their domestic buildings have survived, though inevitably in an altered state today. As previously mentioned, the Vicars' Close at Wells and the smaller example at Chichester give a good idea of the way the secular clergy were housed.

Then, five of the larger monasteries, Chester, Peterborough, Oxford, Gloucester and Bristol, were re-founded as cathedrals for new dioceses created at this time. For a short period Westminster Abbey also became a cathedral, but it lost this status later in the century, becoming, and still being, a collegiate church. Those monasteries which had also been parish churches now became entirely parochial. In some cases the monastic choir at the east end was demolished, leaving only the parochial nave, as at Waltham Abbey, Essex, and Dunstable Priory, Bedfordshire. In other cases the whole church was saved and became parochial, the parishioners generally having to buy the building from the King's Commissioners. Generally the monastic buildings were demolished, but they were sometimes converted to other uses. Some monastic buildings have survived a very chequered history. Saint Nicholas' Chapel, Coggeshall, Essex, the guest chapel of a Cistercian abbey, became a barn for several centuries and was only restored as a church c.1900. It is interesting to note that many of the monastic churches which became parochial at the time of the Dissolution have continued to be called 'abbeys' for centuries since

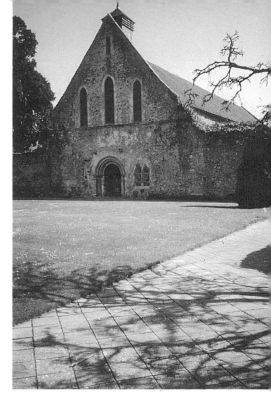

When the Cistercian Abbey of Beaulieu, Hants, was dissolved the monastic refectory became a parish church.

the monks left.

With the ending of the pilgrimages some of the pilgrim chapels fell into disuse and either vanished or were used for other purposes. Some monastic churches became parish churches for the first time. These were generally in towns, where they either replaced an existing parish church or supplemented it to serve an increasing population. Collegiate churches, which were generally also parochial, now became entirely parochial. As with the monastic churches, the collegiate choir was sometimes destroyed or allowed to fall into ruin, as at Howden, Humberside, retaining only the parochial nave. The domestic buildings generally disappeared, but were occasionally converted to other uses.

By far the greater number of monastic churches, though, were less fortunate, and were either demolished immediately after the Dissolution and surrender, or were allowed to become ruinous after the removal of saleable items such as lead from the roofs, or bells. The remaining structures often became used as quarries for the builders of new houses — sometimes by the new owners of the monastic estates, as at Fountains, Yorkshire. The Cistercian abbeys fared particularly badly, since they were generally built in isolated areas where new uses were hard to find. Hospitals and almshouses also suffered, as they were nearly all originally religious foundations, and were included in the general dissolution. Some of them were later re-founded on a new secular basis.

The artistic loss of these years is almost impossible to calculate. It seems in some ways unbelievable that a nation which had until this period been hard at work building and beautifying churches should have indulged in such destruction in a comparatively short time. Vandalism is, of course, not confined to any one period of history. Any building today, standing empty for a few months, is likely to have its windows broken and all fittings of any value stolen. All the same, it still seems strange that in what was still an age of strong religious feeling such destruction, both vindictive and acquisitive, should have taken place. Were the monasteries so unpopular? It is true that over the centuries they had become great landlords, owning about a quarter of the land in England, and that, in the eyes of many people, landlords can do no right. Then again, in the Tudor period, if you wanted to keep your head it was advisable to conform to official policy. The fact remains, though, that the only people to benefit from this early example of nationalisation were the king and his powerful supporters. The ordinary people simply exchanged one landlord for another. Monastic riches were certainly not distributed to the poor.

How did all this affect the parish churches? In a few cases they received fittings from demolished monastic churches, but this represents only a fraction of what was lost. As noted in an earlier chapter, by the end of the Middle Ages many parish churches were 'impropriated' — that is, controlled — by the monasteries. The abbot was patron of the living, and often also became the rector, drawing the tithes and appointing one of his monks as vicar. Now all this was changed. The new patron was the layman who had acquired the abbey and all its estates and rights, and he might also be the rector, receiving the tithes and becoming responsible for the repair of the chancel of the church. There are still some parishes today with a lay rector, originating from this change, but no longer drawing the tithes, which were abolished in the present century. Whether the change was for better or worse depended upon the individual concerned.

Still there were no changes in the form of the services, or in the appearance of the churches. No order had yet been given for the removal of statues of the saints, but it is likely that few new ones were being installed. In 1536 the English Bible was ordered to be placed in churches, and a few churches still have one of these early bibles, now of great value. Because of the shortage of books in the sixteenth century, before printing became general, they were equally valuable then, and for that reason they were generally chained to the lectern or reading desk.

In 1538 the religious shrines were dismantled, the relics destroyed, and

St Peter's Church, Howden, Humberside was formerly a collegiate church. After the dissolution of the college, the parochial nave only remained in use, the collegiate choir being allowed to fall into ruin.

their treasures confiscated. All images considered by the authorities to be superstitious were ordered to be removed from the churches, but the interpretation of this order probably varied considerably in different areas. At Whitchurch Canonicorum, in a remote corner of Dorset, the shrine has survived with its relics intact, although its treasures have long since disappeared. Towards the end of King Henry VIII's reign, a start was made on translating the church services into English from the Latin. In 1547, the year of the king's death, an order was made for the removal of all images in wall or window. This resulted in the limewashing-over of wall paintings — a process which incidentally has often helped to preserve them — and in some loss of medieval stained glass. In the latter case the amount of destruction was probably limited not only by the sentiments of the priest and congregation, but by the high cost of replacing the windows with clear glass. Certainly much early glass did survive this period.

In 1548 the chantries were dissolved and their endowments confiscated. The chapels, though, with their altars removed, remained the property of their founders, who continued to use them as burial places and, increasingly, as family pews. In the same year some of the traditional ceremonies of the Church were abolished and in 1549, the second year of King Edward VI's reign, the First English Prayer Book was issued. The aim of the reformers, led by Archbishop Cranmer, was to give the congregation a greater part in the services, and to do away with the idea of the chancel being the priest's part of the church and the nave that of the congregation. To this end, some of the extremists tried to do away with the chancel screens, but this was not approved by the authorities. Churches were still being used at times for secular purposes, and it was generally thought right to give the chancel some protection. In the 1549 Communion Service, the people were instructed to remain in the nave (by now always furnished with pews) until the Offertory. The priest was to take this first part of the service (the Ante-Communion) from a reading pew in the nave, not from his old stall in the chancel. Then, at the Offertory, priest and people were all to move into the chancel, placing their offerings of money in the oak chest which had to be provided by the parish for this purpose, and for holding the church registers which were ordered to be kept at this time. Many churches still have these chests, with their three locks, one each for the priest and churchwardens so that it could only be opened when all three were present. After making their offerings the communicants remained in the chancel, sitting in the old clergy stalls or in new seats provided for this purpose, for the rest of the service. The chancel was thus to become the Communion room, for both clergy and people.

St John's Church, Oxborough, Norfolk. The south chapel of this church was the chantry chapel of the Bedingfeld family of Oxborough Hall. It was built in the early sixteenth century, and contains the family's fine early Renaissance terracotta monuments. After the Reformation, the Bedingfelds, a Roman Catholic family, retained their ownership of the chapel. The nave of the church is now a ruin, badly damaged by the fall of the spire in 1949, and not rebuilt.

In 1550 an order was made for the removal of the old stone altars, which had generally been fixed close to the east wall of the chancel, and their replacement by wooden communion tables, which were to be set up in the centre of the chancel so that the people could kneel all round them.

In 1552 the Second English Prayer Book was issued. This made more drastic changes in the services, and ordered the abolition of the traditional vestments for the priest, and most of the remaining ceremonies. Further

St Mary Magdalene's Church, Loders, Dorset. The list of incumbents in a church often makes interesting reading. At Loders, the alien priory attached to the church was dissolved during the Hundred Years War, when these establishments were suspected of harbouring French spies, and no more priors were appointed after 1414. In the single year of 1353, during the Black Death, four vicars had to be appointed. On the other hand, Richard Parker held the living from 1533 until 1559 — clearly a survivor!

orders were given for the removal of images, presumably because the previous ones had not always been obeyed.

During the short reign of King Edward VI, inventories were made of the treasures of the parish churches, and most of these were confiscated by the King's Commissioners, leaving the churches stripped to the bare essentials for worship. As had been the case with the monasteries, only the king and his favourites benefited from this pillage, and much of the beauty built up over the centuries was lost. The bewilderment of ordinary people at this time can only be imagined. In 1553 King Edward died, and for the next five years his half-sister Queen Mary Tudor attempted to restore the traditional practices of the Church, and to reconcile the Church of England with the Pope. The fanaticism of her supporters and advisors and the unpopularity of her marriage to the King of Spain probably increased popular support for the aims of the Reformers. At the end of Mary's reign Queen Elizabeth I and her advisors continued the reforming programme, but rather less drastically than had been the case under King Edward VI. At the start of her reign Elizabeth probably hoped to be able to reconcile the by now sharply divided parties in the Church.

Orders were given that no changes were to be made in the churches without due authority. Then a series of Injunctions was issued, which laid down how churches were to be arranged. Extremists were not to be allowed to take the law into their own hands. First, the chancel screens were to be retained. Those which had been removed (without authority) in Edward's reign, and not restored under Mary Tudor, were to be replaced. Like other religious statues, the figures of the Rood were to be removed, as were the parapets to the loft. The reason for this last order

98

The rood screen at St Edith's Church, Coates, Lincs retains its loft. Most of these were removed during the Reformation.

might seem to be obscure until we remember that the loft had often been used to house the choir and organ. In the later Middle Ages church music had become more elaborate, to be 'performed' by a choir. The reformers wanted to restore the congregational singing — apart from an anthem which could be sung by the choir after the third collect at Matins and Evensong. For this reason it was probably thought better to bring the choir down from the loft and to place them in the nave. From this period until the nineteenth century the usual position for the choir was at the west end of the church, either on a raised platform or in a west gallery (sometimes made up from the material of the former rood loft), where they might be accompanied by a local orchestra. The parish clerk still led the singing of the congregation, but now from a seat in the nave, not in the chancel.

St Nicholas' Church, Oddington, Glos. The fine Jacobean pulpit, with its sounding board, demonstrates the importance attached to preaching at this period. Over the chancel arch are painted the arms of King William IV in 1835.

The priest, too, was required to read the offices of Matins and Evensong from a seat in the nave, called the reading pew, not from his old chancel stall, so that the people could see and hear him clearly. By this time practically all churches had pulpits, and eventually it became common for the pulpit, reading pew and clerk's desk to be combined in one piece of furniture, known as the 'three-decker'. In the chancel the altar — a wooden table — was to remain against the east wall except during the Communion service, when it was to be moved into the centre of the chancel and turned round at 90° with its short ends facing east and west, so that the communicants could kneel all round it. Seats for the communicants were sometimes constructed all round the chancel, and the remains of this arrangement can still be seen at the churches of Deerhurst and Hailes, both in Gloucestershire. Towards the end of Queen Elizabeth's reign the altar often came to be left in the central position at all times — indeed the placing of seats across the east wall of the chancel made any other position impossible.

100

Holy Trinity Church, Goodramgate, York. Box pews were installed in many churches after the Reformation, providing some protection from draughts during the long sermons in unheated churches.

At this time, celebrations of the full Communion service became comparatively rare — once a month or so or once a quarter. On other Sundays, the usual morning service consisted of Matins, the Litany and the Ante-Communion, with a sermon, all taken from the reading pew or the three-decker. Sermons were now considered very important and were much longer than they had been in medieval times. The introduction of box pews, which helped to keep out draughts, dates from this period of

101

St Mary's Church, Ellingham, Hants. The tympanum above the screen, which would originally have been painted with the Last Judgement, was repainted after the Reformation with the Royal Arms, and various biblical texts. An enclosed family pew can be seen in front of the screen.

long sermons and generally unheated churches. Pew rents were considered to be a legitimate source of church income, and the pews were allocated by the churchwardens to the various members of the parish. Family pews — sometimes converted chantry chapels — were often furnished very comfortably by their owners, with chairs, tables and fireplaces. This may seem strange to us today, but we should remember the general lack of heating in churches. I suspect that many people who speak disparagingly of the squire's pew with its fireplace would be the first to complain if their own church heating broke down! In Northope, Lincolnshire, the pew belonging to the Hall even had its own dog kennel, known as the Hall Dog Pew. Again, though, we must remember that even

Sunningwell Church, Berks. Comparatively little church building was carried out during the Reformation period, but this porch, showing a mixture of Gothic and Renaissance details, was added to the church in about 1551, reputedly by Bishop Jewel of Salisbury.

in medieval times people used to bring their dogs into church; hence, as we have seen, the original need for chancel screens, with gates. On Sacrament Sundays, at the Offertory, the communicants moved into the chancel as they had done under the Edwardian Prayer Books.

Although the old wall paintings had been whitened over, the church walls were not left bare. Now that more people could read, orders were given for the Creed, the Lord's Prayer and the Ten Commandments to be displayed on the walls. Other biblical texts were sometimes used, and all these might be given decorative borders. The Royal Arms began to appear in churches at this time, but their use does not seem to have been compulsory until after the Restoration of King Charles II.

8

The Seventeenth and Eighteenth Centuries

In the last chapter we looked at the effect of the Reformation on parish churches, taking the story up to the Elizabethan Settlement, and saw how the boom in church building which had characterised the fifteenth and early sixteenth centuries came to a virtual standstill as a result of the uncertainty in the Church. The comparatively few new churches to be built in the later sixteenth and early seventeenth centuries were generally in a traditional late Gothic style, but there was some introduction of Classical details, particularly in features such as doorways, where the round arch re-appeared. The four-centred arch became more flattened, its upper curves being replaced by straight lines, and windows were often square-headed. Chancels were sometimes shorter than they had been in medieval churches, and did not always have chancel arches, but screens were usual. The church of Saint Katherine Cree, in the City of London, built in 1628, shows an interesting mixture of Gothic and Classical architecture.

Inigo Jones' church of Saint Paul, Covent Garden, London, was built in 1631 in a strict Classical style, the first of its kind in England, but on the whole the influence of the Renaissance on parish church design was, until after the Restoration of King Charles II, largely confined to details and to furnishings such as pews, screens, pulpits and font covers, and was often interpreted very freely by local craftsmen.

In the reign of King Charles I some changes were introduced into the Church by William Laud, Archbishop of Canterbury, particularly affecting the altar. He did not like the idea of its being moved about, or left in the centre of the chancel, and felt that these arrangements led to a lack of reverence. Under his orders the altar, still of wood, was to be

Rycote Chapel, Oxon. This chapel, no longer in use, and in the guardianship of English Heritage, is most noted for its seventeenth-century furnishings. The two large canopied pews effectively screen the sanctuary, with its panelled altarpiece, from the nave. In front of the right-hand pew is a combined reading pew and clerk's desk.

St Mary's Church, Leighton Bromswold, Cambs. The church was restored and refurnished by George Herbert, the Rector, from 1627 onwards, for the Prayer Book services. ABOVE *The tower, with Classical-styled windows in a Gothic structure.* BELOW *The communicants' seats in the chancel.*

LEFT *St Mary's Church, East Brent, Somerset. The plaster ceiling to the nave, dated 1637, is similar to those found in houses of the period. It probably covered what was by then an unfashionable medieval timber roof, and helped to keep the church warmer.*

RIGHT *Holy Trinity and St Mary's Church, Abbey Dore, Hereford and Worcs. The surviving part of this Cistercian Abbey church was refurnished in 1634, by the local squire, a High Churchman. The sounding board to the pulpit can be seen through the screen.*

LORDS SUPPER

The Communion Service in the seventeenth and eighteenth centuries. The left-hand picture was printed in 1674, but shows the arrangement more common in the early seventeenth century and the Commonwealth period, with the altar set lengthwise in the chancel, with the communicants kneeling round it. The right-hand picture, printed in 1714, shows the arrangement after the Restoration — a return to the Laudian principles, with the altar back at the east end and the communicants kneeling in front of the rails.

moved permanently back to its old position against the east wall, and enclosed by rails to emphasise its sacred nature. The balusters of the rails were to be closely spaced to keep out dogs. Communicants now knelt at the rail, instead of round the altar, but for a time they continued to remain in the chancel after the Offertory. Some new chancel screens were erected at this period, often showing a mixture of Gothic and Classical design. These changes aroused some opposition, particularly in the Puritan party in the Church, who thought that the Archbishop was trying to re-introduce Roman ideas. In the High Church party, though, the Reformers' fear of ornament, of symbolism, even of imagery, began to recede, and some churches were refurnished at this time with a new dignity. The church at Croscombe, Somerset, is a fine example of Laudian refurnishing.

With the outbreak of the Civil War and the eventual overthrow of the monarchy, the Prayer Book was abolished, and the Puritans controlled the

108

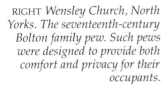

ABOVE *St Mary's Church, Croscombe, Somerset. The medieval church was refurnished in the early seventeenth century, and the photograph shows the upper part of the screen. The barrel roof to the nave is late medieval.*

RIGHT *Wensley Church, North Yorks. The seventeenth-century Bolton family pew. Such pews were designed to provide both comfort and privacy for their occupants.*

SS Peter and Paul's Church, Belton, Lincs. In this seventeenth-century monument, arranged and attired as if attending a Restoration theatre, are Sir John Brownlow, the builder of Belton House, and his 'beloved lady Dame Alicia Brownlow'. The monument was erected by their nephew.

Church. There was a fresh outbreak of iconoclasm, in some areas worse than that of King Edward's reign, stained glass now suffering as well as other ornaments. In view of this it is interesting to see a modern stained glass window in the church at Preston, Dorset, commemorating the writing of the *Pilgrim's Progress*. (One wonders what John Bunyan would have thought of this!) Laud's altar rails were nearly all destroyed, and the Elizabethan chancel arrangements restored. Indeed, in some churches, the chancel ceased to be used, and the altar, or communion table, was placed in the nave.

In spite of these further upheavals a few new churches were built during the Commonwealth period, including those at Plaxtol, Kent, and Staunton Harold, Leicestershire, the latter built as an act of defiance by a High Church and Royalist squire. This church is in a Gothic style, but with furnishings arranged for Prayer Book worship.

After the Restoration of King Charles II most churches were re-arranged in the High Church manner, with the altar moved back against the east wall, and enclosed by rails. During the later seventeenth and the eighteenth centuries many older churches were refurnished with fittings in the Classical style and, with the restoration of more settled conditions,

Chalbury Church, Dorset. This small medieval church was completely refurnished in the eighteenth century. ABOVE The interior, with its three-decker pulpit, classical detailing in the chancel arch, and pews of two types, the taller ones on the south side presumably for those who could afford higher pew rents.

Compton Wynyates Church, Warwicks. The medieval church, in the grounds of Compton Wynyates House, was destroyed in the Civil War, and rebuilt after the Restoration in a Gothic style. Its furnishings, however, are designed for Prayer Book worship. The photograph shows the railed altar.

St James' Church, Cameley, Avon. Galleries were inserted in many older churches in the eighteenth century, to accommodate the growing population.

as well as an increase in population, new churches began to be built again. These were now almost always in the Classical style, and were designed primarily as auditories, the principal aim of their designers being for all the congregation to see, hear and take part in the service. For this reason galleries were introduced, at the west end and sometimes along the side walls, to enable more people to be accommodated without moving them further away from the pulpit. Chancels in new churches were now reduced to small sanctuaries, and screens were less common. The people no longer moved into the chancel at the Offertory, but simply came up to the altar rail to receive Communion, and returned to their seats.

The churches of this period can perhaps best be studied in the City of London, where many were rebuilt by Sir Christopher Wren after the Fire of 1666. As Wren had to build on the old sites, often very restricted and irregular in shape, the plans of these churches vary, but they were all designed on the auditory principle. In spite of demolitions during the nineteenth and early twentieth centuries, when Classical architecture had ceased to be fashionable, and further losses during the Second World War, several of Wren's churches retain their original furnishings. From these it

St Alfege's Church, Greenwich, London was designed by Nicholas Hawksmoor, a pupil of Wren, and built between 1711 and 1714. The photograph shows the impressive entrance portico, of Portland stone.

The Old Chapel, Exeter, Devon. With the growth of religious toleration in the eighteenth century, non-conformist chapels were built in most towns. Such chapels pay less homage to architectural tradition. The photograph illustrates the domestic character of this Baptist chapel.

can be seen that the craftsmanship of this period could be as fine as anything produced in the Middle Ages.

So far we have been looking only at the buildings of the Church of England, but in the seventeenth and eighteenth centuries, with the emergence of a more tolerant attitude in religion, members of other denominations, growing out of the Puritan movement, began to build churches or chapels. These were generally very plain, but some of them contain fine craftsmanship, and, in particular, the Quaker Friends' Meeting Houses have a simple dignity of their own.

During the late sixteenth, and the seventeenth and eighteenth centuries many fine monuments were erected in churches, using some of the skills formerly employed on statues of the saints. Hatchments, bearing the coats of arms of the deceased members of those families entitled to them were carried in the funeral procession and afterwards fixed in the church, providing interesting examples of heraldic painting. Charity boards, recording gifts and bequests, were often put up in churches at this time — a reminder of an age when the Church fulfilled many of the functions of the modern Welfare State.

Tombstones first appeared in churchyards in the seventeenth century, and became far more common in the eighteenth. Many of these are fine

Churchyard monuments became more common in the eighteenth century, and many, like this example from Oxfordshire, are fine examples of carved ornament and lettering.

examples of the mason's craft, with good lettering and other ornament in local stone or slate, and occasionally cast iron, which enhance the setting of the church. The more recent introduction of foreign marbles into churchyards has often been a visual disaster.

As the more extreme puritanism in the Church of England died out, or was transferred to the various Non-Conformist bodies, the fear of superstition receded, and there was a revival of stained glass. Although this eighteenth-century glass does not reach the standard of medieval work, it has a charm of its own. Most churches at this time, though, still had clear glass windows, with crown glass in rectangular leaded panes. For artificial lighting, churches were often provided with fine brass candelabra, although the evening service was usually still held in the afternoon, before it was really dark.

Throughout the eighteenth century, church planning did not greatly vary, although there were some interesting experiments with circular, octagonal, or elliptical churches. There was, for a time, a move to place the pulpit half-way down one side of the nave, or in the centre, directly in front of the sanctuary, but in most cases these arrangements have not survived. Occasionally, too, the font was moved from its traditional site near the main entrance to a position near the sanctuary. Fonts of this period were often of marble, and much smaller than those of medieval times.

At this period there was little appreciation of medieval work, which was considered barbarous — the term 'Gothic' as applied to architecture

St Andrew's Church, Boynton, Humberside. Built in 1768, by John Carr, it shows the influence of the early Gothic Revival. The gallery was originally the squire's pew.

being originally a term of abuse. Repairs and alterations to older churches were generally carried out in a utilitarian manner, which was sometimes less damaging than some of the more self-conscious 'restoration' at which we shall be looking in the next chapter. There were, though, some exceptions. Even Wren occasionally built churches in the Gothic style, such as Saint Mary Aldermary, London, although this may reflect the wishes of his clients rather than his own preference. The nave of Saint Margaret's Church, Kings Lynn, Norfolk, was rebuilt in 1745 after it had been destroyed by the fall of the central tower, in quite a convincing version of Perpendicular Gothic. In the later eighteenth century there was in fact the start of a renewed interest in the Middle Ages and in the Gothic style — part of the cult of the romantic and the picturesque. The ruins of

LEFT *Redland Church, Bristol, Avon, was built between 1740 and 1743 as a proprietory chapel, probably by Strahan and Halfpenny. Although there is no portico, the full-height Ionic order emphasises the importance of the entrance front.*

117

ABOVE *Holy Trinity Church, Teigh, Leics. Rebuilt in 1782 in an early Gothic Revival style, the church shows an interesting experimental plan. The seats face inwards, as in a college chapel. The pulpit and twin reading pews are at the west end, and are backed by a painted 'mock' window, flanked by panels with the Lord's Prayer and the Creed.*

the medieval abbeys, which had for the previous two centuries been regarded simply as useful sources of second-hand stone, now began to be appreciated for their value as landscape features, and several, such as Fountains, Yorkshire, were preserved for this reason. If a landowner did not posses a convenient ruin he might construct one designed to be seen from his house, as the picturesque focus of a landscaped garden.

Some churches were now being built in a revived Gothic style, but this was generally confined to architectural detail. There was no attempt to reproduce the medieval church plan, which would have been considered inappropriate and inconvenient for the services of the time. This early Gothic Revival work is usually rather light-hearted in character, sometimes incorporating features of Oriental origin — reflecting the sentiments which created the Brighton Pavilion. It was to be left to the Victorians to take medieval architecture more seriously.

118

SS Mary, Katherine, and All Saints' Church, Edington, Wilts, is a splendid fourteenth-century church, originally collegiate. It contains this monument, of 1630, to Sir Edward Lewys. The flying cherub is an unusual feature.

St Swithin's Church, Baumber, Lincs. This thirteenth-century church was refurnished in a Gothic Revival style in 1758. The attractive chancel screen could not be mistaken for anything medieval.

9

The Nineteenth and Twentieth Centuries

As we saw at the end of the last chapter, church design in the eighteenth century had evolved into a fairly standard pattern. A church plan had been developed to accommodate the services of the Prayer Book as interpreted at that time. The typical church of the period had a rectangular, often almost square, nave, perhaps with galleries, designed as an auditory church, where all the members of the congregation could see and hear the preacher — the sermon now being considered all-important. At the 'east' end (churches were not always strictly orientated as they had been in the Middle Ages) was a comparatively small sanctuary or altar recess. This was often apsidal — a return, perhaps unconscious, to early Christian practice. The architectural style was generally Classical, but might incorporate some Gothic details. This type of church was essentially practical, designed, as previously stated, to suit the Prayer Book services, yet by the middle of the next century it had been almost entirely superseded by a completely different design, which at first sight would appear to have been far less convenient — the typical Victorian Gothic church. To understand how this change came about we have to look at the social, as well as the religious background to the early years of the nineteenth century.

These changes actually began in the later eighteenth century, although it was not until the early nineteenth century that their full effect was appreciated. I am referring, of course, to the Industrial Revolution and the accompanying changes in agriculture, including the acceleration of the process of enclosure of the open fields and commons. All these developments were accompanied by both an increase in the population as

Freeland Church, Oxon, a country church by J.L. Pearson, built 1869-71, in a traditional Gothic style. Anyone misled from a distance into thinking this was an ancient church would see, at close quarters, many clues identifying this church as a recent building. Semi-circular apses were rare in England by the thirteenth century; the wider band of stone linking the lancets, and the steep pitch of the saddle-back roof to the tower, even the window heads close under the eaves, all suggest a Victorian rather than a medieval date.

121

LEFT *St Stephen's Church, Fylingdales, North Yorks. Built in 1821, this church has Gothic-style windows, but otherwise it is a survival of a common late eighteenth-century design. The bell turret is still Classical. Internally* BELOW *the box pews, west gallery and pulpit halfway down the nave have all survived intact, as a new church was built nearer the village centre in 1868.*

St Matthew's Church, Brixton, London: the stark lines of a Commissioner's Church, built in the Grecian style in 1822 — architect C.F. Porden.

a whole, and a large-scale movement of people from the villages, with their established social order, into the growing industrial towns. This rural depopulation is vividly described in Goldsmith's poem, 'The Deserted Village', and among its other effects it resulted in some village churches falling into decay.

In the growing towns, houses were being built as quickly and cheaply as possible to house the workers in the new factories, and at first nothing was done about building churches for them. The old community life, which had produced churches in the past, was lacking here. Then, early in the nineteenth century, public and official concern started to grow about this situation. In 1820 a Church Building Act was passed, in which Parliament voted one million pounds to be spent on building new churches in the growing towns. Apart from a genuine concern for the religious welfare of the people it was felt by some that churches in these areas might help to counteract any revolutionary tendencies that might be developing there. The memory of the French Revolution was still fresh in people's minds.

The churches built as a result of this Act were known as the Commissioners' Churches. Most of them are in the London suburbs, and the northern and midland industrial towns. They are generally quite large, and rather plain, as they had to be built as economically as possible to hold the maximum number of worshippers. Most of them were designed in the Grecian style fashionable at that time, but occasionally they were in a simple form of Gothic. Internally they followed the eighteenth-century auditory plan, often with galleries.

Apart from this official programme of State-financed church building, a move for building new churches and, where necessary, for enlarging existing churches was growing within the Church itself. In 1818 the Church Building Society had been founded, to raise funds on a voluntary basis for building, enlarging and repairing churches. One condition of a grant from the Society was normally that a certain number of seats should be provided free of pew rents, for those who could not afford them. Other churches were built from funds raised locally by the better-off, for the poor in adjoining parishes, or in the newly developed parts of the original old parishes.

Most of these early nineteenth-century churches were built in the Classical style, but the revived Gothic was growing in favour. At this stage, though, the use of this style was still confined to the architectural details; there was no attempt to reproduce Gothic construction, still less to revive the medieval church plan. Gothic was still treated rather as fancy dress.

Another source of new churches in the early nineteenth century was the building of Proprietary Chapels. These were the result of 'private enterprise', being built neither by the State nor by the Church authorities, but by groups of trustees, who bought the land, built the church and paid the clergyman, hoping to recover their investment from pew rents. As might be expected these chapels were generally built in the wealthier districts, and were served by popular preachers. They were not parish churches, and they did little to help conditions in the growing industrial areas. Most of them eventually became parish churches.

The great change in the attitude to Gothic architecture, and indeed to church planning, which occurred in the nineteenth century was primarily due to the influence of Augustus Pugin, an architect who lived from 1812 to 1852. Pugin was an idealist who made a serious study of medieval art and architecture, and who turned in horror from the industrial cities of his day, looking back to his own idealised vision of the medieval city. Only by returning to this culture was there, according to Pugin, any hope for the world. Pugin was a brilliant draughtsman, and in his book *Contrasts* he drew a series of comparative views, highly exaggerated but convincing at the time, illustrating the same scene in medieval times and the early nineteenth century.

Pugin was originally a member of the Church of England, but finding little sympathy for his revived medievalism he joined the Roman Catholic Church. Here he found things little better. The Roman Church at that time was completely Italianate and Baroque in its culture. Finally, at the end of his life, Pugin suffered a mental breakdown, but not before his ideas had had at last a great influence on English church design. The Gothic detail of the Houses of Parliament is his, as is the Roman Catholic Cathedral of

Christ Church, Kilndown, Kent. The interior of this early Gothic Revival church, by Salvin, was refurnished after 1840 in the style advocated by the Cambridge Camden Society. The furnishings are based on medieval examples.

Saint George, Southwark, although this latter building has been somewhat altered following damage in the Second World War.

In the mid-1830s there was a great revival in the Church of England – the Oxford Movement – started by a group of Oxford scholars, led by John Keble. This movement was not originally concerned with externals such as church architecture, but with doctrine, influenced both by the teachings of the early Christian church, before the Reformation, and by the seventeenth-century High Church movement. It was natural, though, that this should lead on to a revived interest in pre-Reformation church architecture, and it was in this, the Anglo-Catholic wing of the Church of England, that Pugin's ideas eventually found most favour.

The revival at Oxford was followed by one at Cambridge, which was far more concerned with externals such as architecture and ceremonial, and in 1839 the Cambridge Camden Society was founded, to promote the building and furnishing of churches in what was considered a 'correct' Gothic style. This was far removed from the rather light-hearted approach to Gothic architecture which had occurred in the eighteenth century. It was now a matter of principle that churches should be correctly designed as a setting for Catholic worship. An example of this changed attitude can be seen in the church at Kilndown, Kent. It had been built in 1840 in the typical Gothic of the period — Gothic architectural features clothing an auditory church. Soon after its completion, though, it was completely refurnished by the local squire, Alexander Beresford Hope, who was a leading member of the Camden Society. A screen was inserted, forming a separate sanctuary, and all the furnishings are based on genuine medieval models. Originally the walls were covered with painted decoration, but in more recent years these were painted over. The church is still, though, very different from churches that were being built or furnished even twenty years previously. These new ideas, as might be expected, met with some opposition giving rise to fear of 'Popery', but gradually the ideas of the Camden Society came to be accepted throughout most of the Church of England.

St Peter's Church, Leeds, West Yorks. Built in 1841, designed by Chantrell for Dean Hooke, this was one of the first nineteenth-century churches to be built for what were by then considered 'correct' forms of worship. The choir are accommodated in the chancel. The style is late Gothic.

St Thomas' Church, Compton Valence, Dorset. A village church designed by Benjamin Ferrey, in 1838, this is a genuine attempt to reproduce a medieval church in plan as well as in style.

The church at Compton Valence, Dorset, designed by Benjamin Ferrey in 1838, shows an attempt to reproduce the medieval church plan, as well as its details. There was at this time a genuine revival of interest in medieval churches. Books on Gothic architecture appeared, making a serious attempt to date these churches accurately, and 'Ecclesiology' (a coined word meaning the study of church art and architecture) became a popular hobby among both clergy and lay people. The writings of Ruskin, a fervent admirer of Gothic architecture, also encouraged this interest.

The first churches to be built according to the principles of the Camden Society were, like the one at Compton Valence, copied as closely as possible from medieval models, not only in architectural detail, but in their plan. This immediately created problems since, as we have seen, the medieval plan was not really suited to the services of the Prayer Book, and various ways of overcoming this problem had been adopted in the previous three centuries. By the 1840s, though, there was, in the Catholic wing of the Church, a desire for change in the way the services were conducted, making them more like medieval services, or, to be more exact, like what the Victorians imagined the medieval services to have been, which was not always the same thing. One of the mistakes made was to think that services of the type held in cathedrals (which had changed less over the centuries), had also been held in parish churches. Early Victorian churches are therefore based on medieval parish churches, adapted for cathedral services. For instance, it was now considered desirable for the choir of a parish church to be robed, and to sit in the chancel. Unfortunately most medieval chancels, and Victorian ones based on them, are too narrow to hold rows of choirstalls on each side without

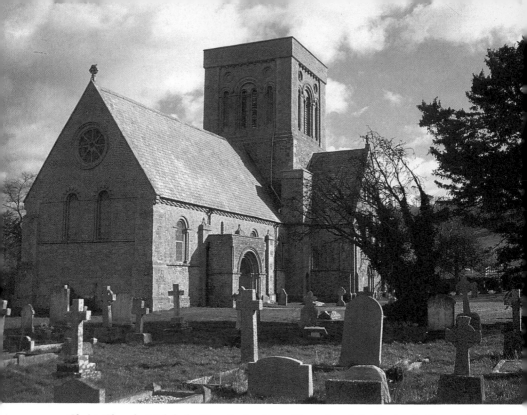

Christ Church, Melplash, Dorset. Another village church by Benjamin Ferrey, this time in the Norman style, which was not generally popular at this period, 1845.

obscuring the view of the altar, which had therefore to be raised on a series of steps, altering the proportions and scale of the chancel.

It was now also considered wrong for the priest to take most of the Communion service, or for that matter, Matins and Evensong, from the reading pew in the nave. He had to have a stall in the chancel, as in medieval times. Sometimes chancel screens were provided in new churches, in accordance with medieval custom, but as it was realised that these would separate the priest from the congregation a compromise was often made by constructing a low screen wall. The three-decker pulpit fell out of favour, and the ancient and honourable office of parish clerk was allowed to die out in many parishes. Box pews were considered incorrect, and not conducive to reverent worship. They were generally superseded by open benches, which were also more suited to the ladies' fashion for crinolines. Pew rents were gradually abolished in favour of a system of voluntary almsgiving, and in place of the old idea of the 'family pew' it became usual in many churches for the men and women to be seated on opposite sides of the nave.

The Victorians particularly disliked galleries in churches, perhaps

128

because they had often been occupied by children who might get up to mischief, or because, if not regularly used, they might become lumber stores. The organ, like the choir, was generally moved from the west gallery and set up near the chancel. In old churches this sometimes resulted in the blocking up of an old chapel.

The church at Rusthall, in Kent, built in 1850 and enlarged later, illustrates the ideas of this period, although here the choir, originally in the chancel, has since been moved out of it. Saint Paul's Church, built in Swanley, Kent, in 1864 shows an attempt to reproduce medieval coloured decoration. Here again the choirstalls are late, and the small sanctuary may not originally have been designed to hold them.

The Ecclesiologists were completely sure of themselves, and put their views forward so forcibly that they were eventually accepted in all sections of the Church. Their propaganda took various forms, one being a series of drawings, obviously inspired by Pugin's *Contrasts*, entitled 'The Deformation and the Reformation', published in 1868 and illustrating the difference between typical church furnishings of the eighteenth and early nineteenth centuries and those advocated by the Ecclesiologists. Although examples of what was shown under 'The Deformation' undoubtedly existed in some areas we cannot help feeling that the Ecclesiologists were guilty of some exaggeration.

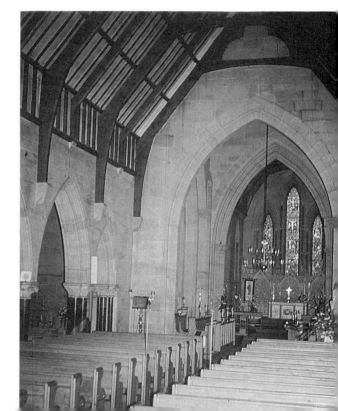

St Paul's Church, Rusthall, Kent. This was built in 1850, and planned for a chancel choir. The dark polished columns of the arcade are typical of the period, as are the open benches in the nave.

Victorian propaganda. 'The Deformation and the Reformation', published in 1868, compared eighteenth and nineteenth-century church design and furnishings, as well as the forms of service. In 'The Deformation', note the three-decker pulpit, galleries and pews. Whether hats were really placed in the font we do not know. In 'The Reformation', note the chancel choir, the chairs — free of pew rents — and the typical Victorian pulpit. Architecturally, the polychrome brickwork and the ventilators in the vaults are also typically Victorian.

Eventually it was realised that churches copied exactly from medieval models did not really suit the services of the nineteenth century, and the better architects of the period began to design churches which, inspired by the Middle Ages, were much more freely planned and designed, using the materials and techniques of their own day. These later Victorian churches can compare well with the best work of earlier centuries. Chancels, for instance, were now designed with adequate space for the choir and for the ceremonial needs of the particular church. The architects were often forceful characters. William Butterfield, whose work can appear to us rather garish due to his use of various coloured materials, did not approve of church heating, except for charcoal braziers which were too unpleasant to be used unless it was really necessary. He also designed seats that were deliberately made more comfortable for kneeling than for sitting.

Indicative of a changing attitude to church design was a statement by Arthur Blomfield, architect of the rebuilt nave of Saint Saviour's Church, Southwark, London (now a cathedral): 'Where convenience is at stake, we

RIGHT *Tue Brook, Liverpool, by G.F. Bodley, and typical of his decorative style. Note the vaulted screen, with loft, and the painting on the walls and roof.*

ought not to be too much confined by the precedent of medieval architecture. Neither our ritual nor our congregations are the same as those for whom our ancient churches were built, and it is scarcely to be expected that if they were exactly suited to the one they would be equally so to the other.' Many of the churches built by such architects as G.E. Street, J.L. Pearson, Gilbert Scott the younger, and G.F. Bodley, were designed for the religious needs of their day, and have stood the test of time as fine pieces of architecture.

The Victorians did not, of course, confine their activities to the building of new churches. They were equally energetic in their approach to restoring and improving old ones. It is true that, by the early nineteenth century, many old churches badly needed repair. This was particularly the case with most of the cathedrals, where the Victorian restorers — notably Sir Gilbert Scott — carried out some remarkable engineering achievements, which probably prevented serious collapse and have preserved these buildings for us. However much we may criticise the Victorian restorers we should not forget these facts.

The trouble was that the Victorians did not confine themselves to carrying out necessary structural repairs. They felt bound to try to make old churches more *correct* architecturally according to their ideas, even if this involved destruction of perfectly sound old work. At this period, the ideal style was considered to be that of the late thirteenth or early fourteenth century, when the Early English style was evolving into the Decorated. When they could afford to do so, the restorers removed all evidence of later work, not only that of the seventeenth and eighteenth centuries which they considered 'pagan', but that of the fifteenth and sixteenth centuries which they considered 'debased'. In place of the

Church of Christ the Consoler, Skelton, West Yorks. The font, by William Burges, who designed the church in 1871-2, although medieval in inspiration, is quite unlike any actual medieval font.

St John the Baptist's Church, Inglesham, Wilts. This charming church, by the Thames, was saved from drastic 'restoration' by William Morris, founder of the Society for the Protection of Ancient Buildings.

destroyed work was put a conjectural restoration of what the church looked, or was thought to have looked like, in the late thirteenth century. Nor was this all. Saxon and Norman work was sometimes condemned as 'barbaric', so that we even find genuine features of this period replaced by imitation thirteenth-century work. All this adds to our problems when trying to date a church. Renaissance churches were now considered to be of little value, and several of Wren's London city churches were demolished, with little opposition.

This destruction and falsification of history did not only occur in the structure of the churches. It was carried out to an even greater extent to the furniture and fittings, since this could be done more cheaply. In many churches we now find Gothic-styled altar rails, or Norman-styled pulpits, where no originals had existed in these periods. All these changes, both in the appearance of the churches and in the forms of service, must, like those of the Reformation four hundred years earlier, have caused great bewilderment to the average congregation. Thomas Hardy's *Under the Greenwood Tree*, describes the effect of such changes in a village church.

Sometimes 'restoration' amounted to a complete rebuilding, perhaps re-using some of the original features. Often, though, the old tower has survived, being more expensive and difficult to demolish. In other cases we find the chancel rebuilt in the nineteenth century, often by a wealthy lay rector who was also probably the local squire.

By the latter part of the nineteenth century, the dangers of this type of restoration, and the damage it had caused, were being appreciated. The Society for the Protection of Ancient Buildings, founded in 1877 by William Morris, protested most strongly and made itself very unpopular with some of the leading church architects in the process, but eventually its principles came to be more generally accepted. Then, early in the twentieth century, and due largely to the work of the late Dr Francis Eeles, was formed the Council for the Care of Churches, and the various Diocesan Advisory Committees, which encouraged a greater appreciation of the real value of ancient churches and of the way they should be treated. This meant respecting the work which had been carried out through all the centuries of a church's existence. Ironically, it was by this time that the good Victorian churches were most in need of protection, since there was in the early twentieth century a reaction against almost anything Victorian.

William Morris and his followers also brought about a revival of craftsmanship, which had been in danger of dying out following the industrial developments of the nineteenth century, when standard Gothic ornament could be mass-produced. The furniture and fittings of the better late Victorian and Edwardian churches, including their stained glass, were often of a very high standard.

At the end of the nineteenth century, and into the twentieth century, Sir J.N. Comper built some fine churches, his free interpretation of Gothic forms sometimes combined with Classical elements. From this period onwards, church architecture continued to develop on similar lines, with greater freedom of design. The Gothic style was no longer considered essential, and we find churches being built in Early Christian, Byzantine, and even Renaissance styles. After the First World War came the first signs of a real break with tradition, and churches began to be built in a style reflecting the new developments in secular architecture. Generally, though, only the architectural style was changed; the plans were still based on the modified medieval layout evolved in the late nineteenth century. This repeated what had happened at the start of the Gothic Revival when, as we have seen, Gothic details had been applied to eighteenth-century plans. By the 1930s, though, other changes began to appear. The John Keble Church, Mill Hill, London, is almost square in plan, and has the choir seated among the congregation, with the organ in a west gallery.

It was not, however, until after the Second World War that a new style of church planning really began to evolve. So far, we have been looking mainly at the buildings of the Church of England, but the influence of the twentieth-century Liturgical Movement has been felt in all denominations. There is, now, as indeed there had been in the sixteenth century, a feeling that the congregation should take a greater part in the service, and this has inevitably had an influence on church design. The long, narrow plan, based on medieval tradition, and the Baroque

St Andrew's Church, Roker, Sunderland, Tyne and Wear, an Arts and Crafts Gothic church, by E.S. Prior, built in 1907. The massive transverse arches, a feature with no real medieval precedent, are typical of Prior's churches. The church contains furnishings by Ernest Gimson, and textiles by Morris and Burne-Jones.

sanctuary, treated rather like the stage in a theatre, with the altar raised up on a flight of steps and surrounded by ornaments, are now considered equally unsuitable. In new churches the altar is generally placed more centrally, and its surroundings kept as simple as possible. It is now often

135

St Martin's Church, Knebworth, Herts, designed by Sir Edwin Lutyens in a free Classical style, with deeply overhanging eaves and pleasant brickwork. The church was started in 1915, but not finished until c.1964, under the care of Sir Albert Richardson.

St Edward the Confessor's Church, Kempley, Glos. The barn-like interior of this church, by Wells, built in 1903, creates a friendly, informal effect, reflecting the Arts and Crafts movement, and the churchmanship of the time.

SS John and Mary Magdalene's Church, Goldthorpe, West Yorks. Built in 1916, by A.Y. Nutt, this is an early example of the use of reinforced concrete in church architecture, in a free Classical style.

hard to tell, unless one knows beforehand, for which denomination a church has been built.

Once again, the influence of current thought is bound to affect the use, and therefore the appearance, of old churches. This is unavoidable — as we have seen, churches have been altered and adapted in every period, but it calls for great care, and we should not forget the lessons of the past. There is a real danger of our own generation being branded as Goths and Vandals when the next change of ideas takes place. Many of the experiments in church planning being advocated today were in fact first tried out in the sixteenth century, and some of them were abandoned as unworkable or as having more drawbacks than merits. This should help us to keep a sense of proportion in these matters. I do not think, though, that we should necessarily be afraid of changes, which may sometimes provide the opportunity to remove some of the unfortunate Victorian and later additions to medieval churches, enhancing both their beauty and their suitability for today's worship. Perhaps it would be advisable, though, to make sure that we do not *destroy* any fittings that we may remove — the next generation may well want to reinstate them.

137

10

Regional variations in English Church Architecture

In the previous chapters I have traced the general history of English church architecture. The changes described took place in all parts of the country, but there were, particularly during the medieval period, some interesting regional variations, and we should now look at these, since they need to be taken into account when we are trying to date and trace the history of a particular church.

The first point to be remembered is what might be called architectural time-lag. New ideas in architecture, as in so much else, started in particular areas and spread out. For instance, as we have seen, the evolution of the Gothic style began in northern France, spreading across the English channel into south-east England, where its influence was first seen in the rebuilding of the choir of Canterbury Cathedral, and from there it spread north and west across the rest of the country.

The influence of the Court was considerable, especially when we remember the political links between the kingdoms of England and France during much of the medieval period. The origin of the Perpendicular style can be traced to the work of the Court masons, and London was probably the focus for much architectural innovation. This was certainly true at the time of the Renaissance; Inigo Jones' church of Saint Paul, Covent Garden being, as we have seen, the first truly Classical-style church to be built in England. Then, we should remember the influence of the cathedrals and the large abbeys. Their leading clerics were often in close touch with the Court and, indeed, with civil and ecclesiastical authorities on the Continent — often sources of new ideas in architecture. From the cathedrals and abbeys these new ideas were sometimes passed on to those parish churches under their control. For instance, the fine fifteenth-century tower of Marnhull Church, Dorset, shows strong Somerset influence in its design, and was probably the

Borrowdale Church, Cumbria. In remote areas such as the Lake District, many of the churches are simple unpretentious buildings, little influenced by current architectural fashions.

139

result of its impropriation by Glastonbury Abbey. In contrast to all this, we find, in remote country areas, very plain, simple churches with few architectural pretensions.

Another important influence on local style was the economic prosperity of an area at different times. During the later Middle Ages much of the wealth of England was derived from the trade in wool, first in the fourteenth century in raw wool, and later, during the fifteenth and early sixteenth centuries, in woven cloth. In those areas, such as parts of the

Holy Trinity Church, Long Melford, Suffolk. This splendid fifteenth-century church reflects the prosperity of East Anglia at the height of the wool and cloth trades. Note the use of brick in the stair turret.

Midlands, where the trade in raw wool was greatest, we find some very fine work of the fourteenth century; while in East Anglia and the Cotswolds, centres of the weaving trade, the best churches were built later. Indeed in these areas many churches were completely rebuilt in the fifteenth and early sixteenth centuries. Economic conditions at later

141

The ironwork to the door, believed to be of Viking origin, of St Helen's Church, Stillingfleet, North Yorks.

periods also determined, as we shall see, the extent to which medieval churches were altered, refurnished, or restored and rebuilt in succeeding centuries.

Another influence, which became rather less important over the centuries, was that of race. In Saxon and Norman times, some churches in the east and west parts of England respectively, show evidence of Scandinavian or Celtic influence, particularly in their ornament.

Perhaps, though, the main factor affecting local style has been the geology of the area, governing the availability of the various building materials, at least until the nineteenth-century developments in transport made it possible to move building materials relatively cheaply over wide areas. For the cathedrals, large abbeys and other rich churches good stone might be imported from some distance, particularly where it could be brought by water. In southern England, in Norman times, Caen stone was shipped across the Channel. Stone was also imported, for use in Hampshire, for some of the greater churches, from the Isle of Wight. In the fourteenth century, oak trees for the construction of the Octagon at Ely Cathedral, Cambridgeshire, were brought by waggon from many parts of the country, the Fens providing little timber of the size required.

The smaller parish churches, though, had to be built of whatever materials were available locally. Where there was no good local stone, and it had to be imported, it was used quite sparingly for quoins, window tracery and other essential items, often providing interesting contrasts in texture with the local material used for the general walling. The best and

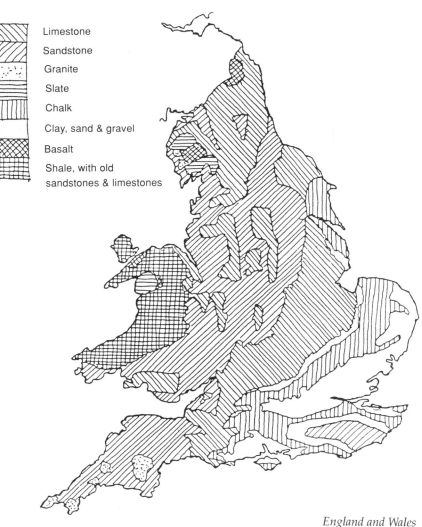

	Limestone
	Sandstone
	Granite
	Slate
	Chalk
	Clay, sand & gravel
	Basalt
	Shale, with old sandstones & limestones

England and Wales
Simplified geological map showing principal building stones

most easily worked stone was found in the belt of limestone extending across England from Dorset through the Cotswolds, Northamptonshire and the East Midlands to Lincolnshire. Churches in these areas show masonry of a high standard, but the stones themselves vary in their durability. Some have weathered well, but others have suffered badly from decay, particularly after the increased atmospheric pollution of the industrial age, necessitating much subsequent restoration. Unfortunately the Victorians, in their restorations, made much use of Bath stone in many

143

areas, and this in its turn has suffered in a similar way in polluted atmospheres.

Sandstones, found in general in a belt northwest of the limestone, were generally more difficult to work, and churches in these areas have less in the way of carved ornament. Like the limestones, sandstones vary in their durability. In a few areas granite was the principal building stone, and this gave rise to simple, rather rugged forms. Areas lacking in these principal stones had, as we shall see, to make do with other, less suitable materials, which had an important effect on building design.

Local geology also gave rise to certain centres of craftsmanship. One of these was the Purbeck Marble industry of southeast Dorset. The 'marble' was in fact a hard limestone which takes a polish, and it was used for features such as column shafts and carved effigies, and exported from the Isle of Purbeck to many parts of the country during the thirteenth century, resulting in a period of prosperity for the area. Similarly, the alabaster quarries of Derbyshire and Nottinghamshire gave rise to another local industry, the production and export of alabaster carvings, both for altarpieces and for funeral effigies. This developed rather later than the Purbeck Marble industry, in the fourteenth, fifteenth and early sixteenth centuries.

Let us look now at some parts of Britain showing the most distinct regional characteristics in church architecture.

St Breaca's Church, Breage, Cornwall. The rather severe granite exterior of this church hides some good late nineteenth-century fittings by Sedding, and medieval wall paintings.

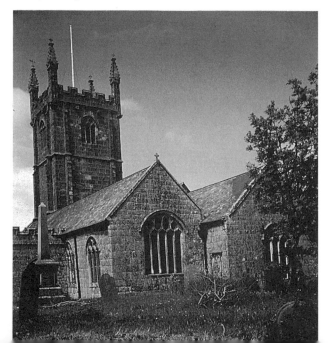

St Peter's Church, Tiverton, Devon. The soft limestone used for this church made possible the elaborate carvings of the porch. Unfortunately, though, this stone weathered badly, and there has been much recent renewal.

Devon and Cornwall

In these counties the principal building stones are red sandstone, granite and Beer stone (a soft cream-coloured limestone). The sandstone, and to an even greater extent the granite, provided durable walling material but were not easily worked or carved. The Beer stone, obtained in south Devon, was often used for these details. Many of the churches of this region are rather severe and plain in character, but there were some notable exceptions. For instance at Tiverton, Devon, and Launceston, Cornwall, the churches show some elaborate carved detail. At Tiverton, the soft stone used for this has decayed badly, necessitating much recent renewal.

145

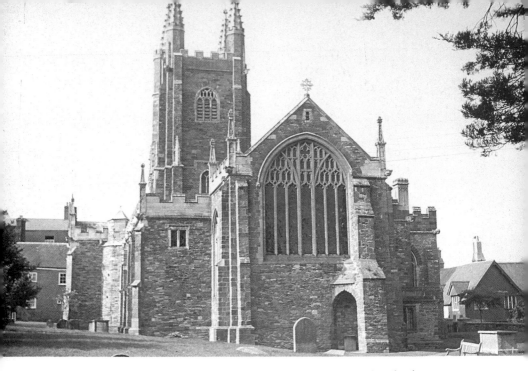

St Mary's Church, Totnes, Devon, the fifteenth-century church of a prosperous Devon town, built of the local red sandstone. The bold pinnacles of the tower are typical of the county.

Church towers generally are rather plain, with battlemented parapets and projecting stair turrets. Spires are rare, but there is a small group of towers with lead-covered spires near Exmoor. On plan, the churches of Devon and Cornwall rarely have clerestories. The aisles, often nearly as wide as the nave and extending for the full length of the chancel, may have separately pitched roofs, providing two or three gables at the east end. The typical roof of the region is of the trussed rafter form, sometimes with curved braces to the rafters, forming a 'wagon' or 'barrel' roof. Most of these were originally plastered, divided into panels by moulded beams, but in some churches this plaster has been removed in nineteenth-century restorations.

Perhaps to compensate for the general simplicity of the stonework, Devon churches in particular often contain very fine woodwork. Bench-ends, generally flat-topped, may be richly carved, and screens, with vaulting supporting the loft and sometimes retaining their original colour, are often of a very high standard. The survival of so many screens in Devon may be partly due to the fact that the county was, in the sixteenth and seventeenth centuries, the home of Royalist and High Church sympathies, and indeed supported an early rebellion against the First English Prayer Book, describing its services as 'No better than a

St Pancras' Church, Widecombe-in-the-Moor, Devon. A typical West Country interior, with unclerestoried nave and aisles of equal height, and plastered barrel roofs.

Christmas game'. Fewer screens have survived in the more Puritan county of Cornwall.

The Chalk Downlands and the London Basin

The downlands and the sands and clays of the London basin cover parts of the counties of Surrey, Sussex, Kent, Wiltshire, the Chilterns, extending to parts of East Anglia, and of Wessex, although these latter areas will be looked at later.

Chalk is not a particularly durable material. If used for walling it was almost always plastered, and it is more often used for the inner wall faces only. Sometimes clunch, a rather harder form of chalk, was used, especially for mouldings and dressings, but the principal walling material in these areas was flint. Flint is a very hard, durable material, but it can only be used for general walling. For quoins and other details, stone had to be used. In the humbler churches the flints were used uncut, as they were found, and this rough flint walling was generally plastered. In many cases, though, this plaster has been removed in nineteenth-century restorations. In the larger and richer churches the flints were sometimes cut, or knapped, to show the dark polished interior, and to produce a

St George's Church, Arreton, Isle of Wight. Mainly of the fourteenth century, the catslide roof over the north aisle, and the dormer window (originally to light the rood), give the church a homely, almost domestic character.

flush wall finish. In some parts of Surrey, Sussex and west Kent we find a detail known as 'galletting', where fragments of stone or flint are pushed into the wide mortar joints, presumably to reduce the risk of the mortar shrinking and cracking.

Towers were generally rather plain, and had either parapets or timber shingled spires. Sometimes there was only a timber bell-cote rising from the west end of the nave roof. In order to avoid the need for quoin stones, round towers were sometimes built. Many of the churches in these areas were quite small and simple, reflecting the populations and sizes of the parishes. Indeed, during the later Middle Ages many downland villages were depopulated and disappeared at times of economic recession.

These little churches do, though, have rather a pleasant homely character. In Sussex, and in parts of Hampshire and the Isle of Wight, the aisles were often roofed as 'catslides', continuing the slope of the nave roof, without a clerestory, giving the buildings an almost domestic character. Towers in these areas were sometimes finished with a low, pyramidal cap — half way to a spire.

Much of the area we are looking at surrounds London, and in the nineteenth century, as London spread out and the railways made

St John Lateran Church, Hengrave, Suffolk. Round towers are found in areas, such as parts of East Anglia, where stone was scarce, and flint the main building material. The circular tower plan avoided the need to construct stone quoins.

commuting easier, many of these originally small, simple churches were enlarged or rebuilt to suit the growing population. What had been villages in Surrey, Kent and Middlesex, and even parts of Berkshire and Buckinghamshire had now become London suburbs. Few of their churches have survived unaltered; in many cases only the tower of the medieval church now remains.

East Anglia

While the chalk belt extends to parts of East Anglia, other areas here consist of clay and gravel, and there was little good building stone available locally. This was, though, an area of great wealth in the later Middle Ages, due partly to the cloth industry, but also to the opportunity for trade with Europe provided by ports at the river estuaries. Norfolk and Suffolk and, perhaps to a lesser degree Essex, have some of the finest late medieval churches in England, many having been completely rebuilt in the fifteenth century.

Flint was the normal walling material, imported stone being used for quoins and other details and, where it could be afforded, for elaborate

149

St Mary's Church, Layer Marney, Essex. Standing next to the famous Layer Marney Towers, this church was built in the early sixteenth century, using the local brick, which was by then becoming a fashionable building material.

flushwork patterning with the knapped flints. However, brick was also increasingly used for walling after its reintroduction into England from Europe in the thirteenth century. Essex in particular has some fine brick towers. There is some evidence that early brickwork was plastered, to imitate stone, but by the end of the Middle Ages brick was being accepted as a facing material in its own right, leading to the elaborate brickwork of the Tudor period.

Church naves were generally clerestoried, and as in Devon and Cornwall, East Anglia is noted for its church woodwork. The roofs are particularly fine, and it was in this area that the hammer-beam roof was most fully developed, often decorated with flights of carved angels. Screens were also elaborately carved, but unlike those of Devon they were not usually vaulted below the lofts. Bench-ends were generally of the 'poppy head' form. Timber was also sometimes used for complete towers, as distinct from bell-turrets, and Essex has some interesting examples, as at Blackmore and Marks Tey.

The prosperity of East Anglia suffered a sharp decline in the eighteenth century, when the cloth trade died out here, and there was no great industrial development in the nineteenth century. For this reason, many

St Andrew's Church, Marks Tey, Essex. Another Essex church, where, due to lack of good building stone, the base of the tower was built of brick, and the upper part of timber. The porch is also of timber-framed construction. The little 'needle' spire is typical of Essex and Hertfordshire.

of the churches, especially in villages rather than towns, retain much of their medieval character and atmosphere, having escaped both eighteenth and nineteenth-century alterations. In many cases a large, magnificent and unspoiled church now serves a tiny village or hamlet — a delight for the student of church architecture, but a major headache for the Church authorities when it comes to maintaining and preserving the fabric, a subject we shall be considering in a later chapter.

Kent

Parts of Kent lie on the chalk, but the county also includes areas of Greensand and of clay. In the Greensand areas the principal stone is Kentish Rag, quite a hard stone, but difficult to work, and used mainly for general walling. For window tracery and other moulded work a softer clunch-like stone was sometimes used, which was less durable and has often been replaced with Bath stone in nineteenth-century restorations. In spite of the proximity of this county to the Continent, brickwork does not appear in many medieval Kent churches.

151

Regional Variations

In the towns there are some fine late medieval churches, such as those at Tenterden and Maidstone (the latter being collegiate). but most of the village churches are rather plainer and humbler, reflecting the more modest prosperity of the Kentish yeomen rather than the opulence of the wool magnates of East Anglia and the Cotswolds. In plan the Kentish churches, like those of Devon and Cornwall, are often without clerestories, the nave and aisles having parallel pitched and gabled roofs. The most popular roof design is of the trussed rafter and crown-post form, this also being typical of the late medieval Kentish yeomen's houses. A particular form of window tracery, producing a honeycomb effect, is found in the county, and is sometimes known as Kentish tracery.

There are a number of timber, shingled spires in the county, but the more typical Kentish church tower is simply battlemented, with a projecting stair turret. Like those in the other Home Counties, the churches of Kent, particularly in areas near to or readily accessible from London, have had a considerable amount of nineteenth-century restoration, enlargement and rebuilding, and except in remote areas such as Romney Marsh it is rather rare to find many medieval furnishings surviving.

The Cotswolds

This area includes much of Gloucestershire and parts of Wiltshire and Oxfordshire. The principal building materials were a series of fine oolitic limestones, used not only for walling but for the stone slate roofs which give the district much of its character. Most of the limestones were. easy to work, and the area is characterised by its fine masonry, including sculptures and other carved and moulded work. The durability of many of these stones has assisted the survival of much medieval work.

Some of the village churches are quite small, humble buildings, retaining much Norman and some Saxon work. Some, like the one at Elkstone, have not been enlarged since Norman times, indicating a fairly static population level. Spires are comparatively rare, most towers having simple parapets or gabled saddleback roofs. The Cotswolds are most noted, though, for the fine series of large 'wool' churches, built or rebuilt in the fifteenth century by rich wool and cloth merchants, or by the trade guilds; churches such as those at Cirencester, Northleach, Fairford and Chipping Camden.

It is interesting to compare these churches with equivalent,

SS Peter and Paul's Church, Northleach, Glos. One of the great Cotswold fifteenth-century 'wool' churches. The photograph shows the porch with the high quality masonry made possible by the good building stone of the area.

contemporary ones in East Anglia. First, as we have seen, the general availability of good stone in the Cotswolds resulted in far more detailed and ornamental stone masonry than was general in East Anglia. Towers and porches in particular were often enriched with stone traceried panelling. On the other hand, the woodwork in the Cotswolds is rarely as fine as that in East Anglian churches. Roofs are generally simpler, the typical form being a flat-pitched roof, divided into panels by moulded beams. Screens and bench-ends, though showing fine craftsmanship, do not often reach the standards of those in East Anglia, or indeed in Devon. One typical feature of Cotswold churches is a window above the chancel arch, probably to light the Rood.

On the whole, fewer churches in the Cotswolds retain their medieval interiors unaltered than is the case in East Anglia. There has been rather more Victorian refurbishing, probably the work of wealthy Victorian squires living in the fine manor houses typical of the area. Two churches, though, at Deerhurst and Hailes, retain the remains of their Elizabethan chancel furnishings, with seats all round the chancel, originally surrounding the altar.

Wessex including Somerset, parts of Dorset, and East Hampshire

This area contains a considerable variety of building materials, good limestones of the Cotswold type, a softer Blue Lias stone, Greensand, chalk and clay in the river valleys.

In parts of Somerset and northwest Dorset the Cotswold-type stone produced churches of similar character to those of the true Cotswolds. Somerset in particular (another centre of the wool and cloth trade) has a series of especially fine towers, with pinnacled parapets, and wall faces enriched with panelled decoration and sculpture. One cannot help feeling that these were often the results of inter-parochial rivalry. These churches also often have some good interior woodwork. In other parts of Somerset the Blue Lias stone was used for walling, but as this was less easily worked, other imported stones were often used for details. The churches on the chalk downlands of Wessex were, as described elsewhere, generally of flint. In the Isle of Purbeck a hard grey-toned stone was and still is quarried, suitable for general walling, but not very easily worked. As in the Blue Lias areas, other softer stones were often used for details.

St James' Church, Winscombe, Avon. The fifteenth-century tower, with its pierced parapet. Before the reorganisation of the counties, this village was in Somerset, where fine towers abound.

Regional Variations

In the Isle of Portland a particularly good quality limestone was quarried, and by the later Middle Ages this was being exported, by sea, to other parts of the country, being used extensively by Wren for his work in London after the Fire of 1666, including Saint Paul's Cathedral and most of the rebuilt City churches.

The roofs of these Wessex churches were often of the arch-braced collar-beam type, but other forms are found, including the barrel or waggon roof typical of Devon and, in later churches, the flat-pitched panelled roof. In Dorset, many churches were considerably restored and refurbished in the nineteenth century, with often only the tower surviving a complete rebuilding. This may be the result of a period of relative rural prosperity in the later nineteenth century, following one of great depression earlier in the century, when the poor condition of the Dorset farmworkers became a national scandal. Two medieval churches, at Chalbury and Winterborne Tomson, retain complete eighteenth-century furnishings, but these are exceptions to the general rule.

St Oswald's Church, Lower Peover, Cheshire. Except for the tower, this church is built of timber framing, giving it a distinctive character.

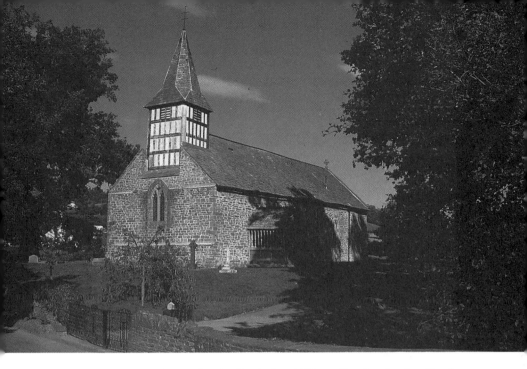

St Bartholomew's Church, Vowchurch, Hereford and Worcs. The church, of medieval origin, was altered c.1613 producing, externally, a single-span roof. The timber-framed bell turret is typical of this area.

The West Midlands and the Welsh Border Counties

Here the principal building stone is sandstone, much of it a deep red colour which gives a distinct character to the churches, ranging from Chester Cathedral and large town churches such as that at Leominster, to some quite small parish churches in the villages. To anyone accustomed to the cream-coloured limestone of the south this red sandstone may give the churches rather a heavy, even depressing character, but we should remember that in medieval times they would probably have been limewashed and decorated internally, their present appearance being largely the result of Victorian scraping. In the smaller churches, built of rubble, the interiors are more likely to retain their original plaster coating. It is in the larger churches, built of ashlar stone, that the dark red colour often dominates the building, an effect intensified in churches containing much dark nineteenth-century stained glass.

In parts of this area, though, there was little good stone locally available, and timber was used extensively for towers, and occasionally for complete churches. Sometimes the timber framing is weatherboarded externally, but in other cases it is exposed, giving these towers quite a 'domestic' character.

157

St John's Church, Shobdon, Hereford and Worcs. The church of c.1752, replacing a Norman building, shows a mixture of Gothic and oriental elements: the fanciful interior completely belies the plain exterior.

In parts of the Welsh border country the Norman work shows a Celtic, or perhaps Scandinavian character, producing striking, indeed at times grotesque animal and figure sculpture, best seen in the remarkable church at Kilpeck, Hereford and Worcestershire. Not far away from this, at Shobdon, the remains of a similar church, demolished in the eighteenth century, were re-erected as an 'eyecatcher' or folly on a nearby hill, while the church which replaced it is a remarkable example of the early Gothic Revival, showing Oriental influence rather reminiscent of the Royal Pavilion at Brighton. Several of the old churches in this region retain attractive eighteenth-century furnishings, and seem largely to have escaped Victorian restoration, probably reflecting the economic history of the area.

The East Midlands

Much of this area lies within the limestone belt, and as would be expected there are fine churches showing good quality stonework, similar to that found in the Cotswolds. In particular, the stone spires are typical, most of them dating from the fourteenth century, when the wealth of the area, derived from the raw wool trade, was at its greatest. These counties also profited from trade with the Low Countries, channelled through the ports of Kings Lynn and Boston, both of which towns have exceptionally fine churches. The churches of the East Midlands were often of cruciform plan, a form which can still be traced in spite of later extensions. As in the Cotswolds, stone slates were sometimes used for church roofing, harmonising particularly well with the walls. Internally, as we have also seen in the Cotswolds, the roof construction was generally fairly simple, the low-pitched tie-beam roof being popular in the later Middle Ages.

It is interesting that in the area around Northampton are two of the finest surviving examples of Saxon church architecture — the remarkable basilican church at Brixworth, and the massive tower at Earls Barton, with its pilaster strip decoration. Around Nottingham, as previously noted, fine examples of alabaster carving can be found, mainly in monuments but occasionally in a surviving altarpiece.

St Mary and All Saints' Church, Willoughby-on-the-Wolds, Notts. One of the series of fine fifteenth-century alabaster monuments in this church. Nottingham was a centre of the alabaster industry in late medieval and Tudor times.

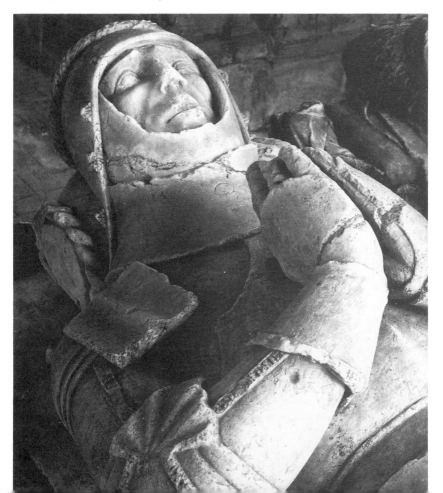

The Northern Counties

In medieval times, these counties were generally more sparsely populated than those further south and, as would be expected, in many areas the churches are relatively fewer in number. In parts of the Yorkshire Dales one church would be built to serve a group of parishes, and such churches are often rather plain in character. At the other extreme, in a city such as York, the density of the parish churches rivals that at Norwich, and must reflect the local wealth of the community.

In much of the area a carboniferous limestone, relatively easy to work, alternates with millstone grit, a very hard sandstone, while in the Lake District is found a hard grey-green slate, and some red sandstone — all these materials influencing the design of the churches. In these northern areas there was, of course, much industrial growth in the nineteenth century, and many of the medieval town churches were extensively restored, enlarged and rebuilt. Many of these towns, though, had been quite prosperous market towns in medieval times and had fine churches, such as that at Halifax, West Yorkshire. Those that survived among the factories and the nineteenth-century civic buildings and housing became blackened with soot. In recent years many of them have been cleaned, revealing an almost forgotten beauty.

Nearer the Scottish border the churches are often found to retain a defensive character, with massive towers, throughout the medieval period — a reminder of the unsettled political situation until the Union of England and Scotland under King James I.

When we think of Yorkshire and the North, though, perhaps their greatest contribution to church architecture is to be found in the splendid series of Cistercian abbeys, nearly all now in ruins. As we have seen in earlier chapters, the Cistercians generally chose remote, isolated sites for their abbeys, and the sparsely populated areas of Yorkshire suited them well. The land was also well suited for sheep rearing (it was the monks' principal source of income, and during the Middle Ages they developed into wealthy sheep farmers, helping to establish the woollen industry in this part of England). The isolated positions of these monasteries meant that the churches were rarely able to continue in use after the Dissolution, and they were used largely as quarries by local people until the revival of interest in medieval architecture in the nineteenth century.

As we have seen, the influence of the Renaissance was first felt in London, and in the more remote areas of the country Classical styled churches only began to be built after the Restoration of King Charles II. From this period onwards local characteristics became less marked. The

St Mary's Church, Whitby, North Yorks. Adjoining the ruins of Whitby Abbey, the parish church, of medieval origin, was altered and refurnished in the eighteenth century. Note the rather domestic-looking windows, inserted in the eighteenth century to light the galleries and pews.

Georgian style, in churches as in houses, varied little in different districts except in its use of local materials. Even in this respect there was now more attempt at uniformity. When stone replaced brick as the fashionable building material in the later eighteenth and early nineteenth centuries those who could not obtain local stone, or afford to import it, would cover their brick buildings with plaster, often marked out to imitate ashlar stone. Finally, in the nineteenth century, when mass-production and cheaper transport meant that building materials could be moved over great distances, local style in English church architecture practically disappeared, although there was some attempt to revive it under the influence of the Arts and Crafts movement.

161

Changes of building material, blocked and inserted openings, and evidence of destroyed features can all help in working out the history of a church, in this instance, St Osyth's Priory, Essex.

11

Looking at a Church, the exterior

From what we have seen in previous chapters it should be clear that a church cannot always be dated simply by its apparent architectural style and details. A Gothic church, for instance, may be a genuine medieval building, an example of seventeenth-century Gothic Survival, Gothic Revival work of the eighteenth, nineteenth or early twentieth century or, as is often the case, a medieval church which has been altered and restored in later centuries. 'Restoration' can cover anything from careful and conservative repair, wholesale renewal in a style faithfully copying the original work, to renewal of features in a style considered to be more 'correct' by the antiquarians of the time. The degree of restoration can also vary between fairly superficial repairs, and practical rebuilding, perhaps retaining some features from the original church. In many cases it will be found that even when an old church has been otherwise completely rebuilt the medieval tower has survived, being the most substantial part of the structure and the most difficult to demolish.

Churches built in the Classical style do not usually present so many problems. This style developed from the late seventeenth-century, or 'Queen Anne' style, typified by the work of Wren, through the more formal Palladian style of the eighteenth century, to the Greek Revival of the early nineteenth century, after which it was generally superseded by Gothic Revival work. The Classical style was generally unpopular in the later nineteenth century, although at the end of that century and in the early twentieth century there was a brief 'Georgian' revival, contemporary with a free interpretation of Gothic, influenced by the Arts and Crafts movement.

Bearing all these things in mind, let us look at a typical parish church and note the features which can help in its dating. First, the location of the church in its town, village or suburban setting should be considered. An old church is likely to be in the oldest part of the settlement, but there will be exceptions. From the medieval period onwards there have been cases of villages or towns being moved from their original sites — usually the

The Old Church, Oborne, Dorset. The chancel is all that survives of the old church, the rest having been demolished when another church was built nearer the new centre of the village in 1862.

result of economic changes, but sometimes following an outbreak of plague or other disease. In many cases the church remained on its old site, perhaps being eventually abandoned and replaced by a new building nearer the population. More recent developments in the area may now surround such an old church with new buildings, resulting in its being restored to use, such as happened at the old church at Chingford, Essex, which now serves a comparatively new residential area.

The churchyard should be studied. As we have seen, although churchyards were used for burial from early medieval times, actual gravestones were rare before the late seventeenth or early eighteenth centuries. An old parish church, or a church rebuilt on its old site, is likely to be surrounded by gravestones from these and later centuries. By the mid-nineteenth century, in towns at least, churchyard burials were becoming less common, and churches of this date are less likely to be surrounded by gravestones. Of course, there has in recent years been a wave of clearing churchyards of gravestones to facilitate maintenance, but even where this has happened some may remain, perhaps refixed round the outer walls, or re-used as paving stones.

While in the churchyard, note any lychgate. A few medieval ones have survived, but being mainly timber structures they are subject to decay, and far more will be found to be of nineteenth or twentieth century date. In a very few cases a medieval lychgate survived the rebuilding of the church, as at Saint George's Church, Beckenham, Kent. Later lychgates, although in a traditional style, are generally easy to identify. Apart from the obvious newness of the timbers, they are often dated, being a popular form of memorial. A lychgate with a resting slab for the coffin is likely to be medieval.

164

ABOVE *St Mary's Church, Monnington-on-Wye, Hereford and Worcs. The lych gate, dating, like the church, from the seventeenth century.*

BELOW *Fourteenth-century ironwork on the south door of St Mary's Church, Meare, Somerset.*

Having passed through the churchyard, look at the church itself, and note first the walling material. Until the nineteenth century brought mass-production and cheaper transport, churches, like houses, were generally built of easily available material. Is the stone local? If not, could it have been brought from a distance relatively easily, perhaps by water? Is it laid in the local traditional manner? This will involve comparing it with other local buildings of known date. In the Middle Ages even rubble stone was generally coursed, or 'brought to courses'. True random rubble was then

LEFT *St Margaret's Church, Marton, Lincs. The church has a Saxon tower, and a Norman chancel arch. The south aisle, with its Perpendicular-style windows, dates from the fifteenth century. Most churches, like this one, will be found to contain work of several centuries. The line of an earlier steeply pitched roof can be seen against the wall of the tower.*

BELOW *St Peter's , Bengeo, Herts. A Norman two-cell church with an apsidal sanctuary. Most of the windows are later medieval insertions. A blocked priest's door can be seen in the wall of the sanctuary.*

St Andrew's Church, Cheddar, Somerset. The straight joint at the west end of the aisle indicates that this and the tower are of two builds.

only used for very humble buildings, but in the nineteenth century it became fashionable, often accompanied by a rather hard, unpleasant pointing. Also, in medieval times, much rubble walling was originally covered with a thin coat of plaster, or with repeated coats of limewash, and although these were often stripped by Victorian restorers, who mistook this covering for eighteenth-century work, traces of it can sometimes be seen.

Changes in the masonry work, either in the actual materials or in their method of laying, can indicate alterations and extensions to the original building, helping us to put together the development of the church. Incidentally, as previously noted, while herringbone masonry is sometimes considered to be proof of Saxon date, this is not always the case. It was certainly used in post-Conquest work, but is unlikely to be later than the Norman period, unless 'copied' in recent centuries.

168

It is now being discovered that more churches of Saxon date have survived, albeit altered, than was once thought, and it is an interesting exercise to try to find evidence for this. As we have seen, many Saxon churches were very tall in relation to their length and breadth, and these proportions in the church, or, more often, the central part of it, may indicate a Saxon origin. Traces of the original 'long and short' work in the quoins, perhaps hidden by later aisles, or of the flat pilaster strips of ashlar stone, on rubble walling, can also indicate Saxon work, even though all features such as windows and doors have been changed.

Straight joints, like changes in masonry, show where a building has been enlarged or altered. Sometimes we shall find evidence of a church having been *reduced* in size, reflecting a fall in the local population. Built-up arcades from former aisles may be seen in what is now an external wall, or remains of old footings from demolished buildings may survive. It is also worth looking for evidence of former roof lines — often seen on the east wall of a west tower. In the later Middle Ages the earlier, more steeply pitched roofs were often replaced by ones of flatter pitch, this sometimes accompanied by raising the nave walls to accommodate a clerestory. It was also usual in the later Middle Ages to replace the small

Fifteenth-century flint flushwork at the base of the porch, St Mary's Church, Woodbridge, Suffolk.

St Mary's Church, Stoke-sub-Hamdon, Somerset. A Norman church, with medieval alterations. The photograph shows one of the original Norman windows, with later insertions of the thirteenth and fifteenth centuries.

Saxon and Norman windows with larger ones, but the remains of the original windows, now built up, can sometimes be seen, and the insertion of later windows is sometimes indicated by disturbance of the masonry. It will also often be found that a richly ornamented Norman doorway has been refixed in a later aisle wall.

As we have seen, most medieval churches contain work of successive periods, few remaining unaltered from their first building. The main exceptions to this were in the late fifteenth and early sixteenth centuries, at the height of the wool and cloth trade, when some churches were completely rebuilt on such a scale that no subsequent enlargement became necessary. If we find a Gothic church, particularly one apparently of an earlier period, all of one style and showing considerable uniformity of design, we should suspect that it may be Victorian, or at least a heavily restored building. The Perpendicular style was not generally popular in the Victorian period, and confusion is less likely with churches in this style.

In Victorian and later restoration work the original stone was not

LEFT *One of the original windows in the small Norman church of All Saints', Sutton Bingham, Somerset. Skelton Old Church, North Yorks* RIGHT *by contrast, is an eighteenth-century building. The tooled masonry, and the round-headed window with Gothic-style glazing, are typical of this period.*

always used; indeed, it was often no longer being quarried. Bath stone was very popular at this time and was used in many areas far from its original quarries. It can be identified by the rather strong yellow colour to which it weathers, and, unfortunately, by its susceptibility to damage from atmospheric pollution. In this connection, it might seem easy to distinguish between genuine medieval work and nineteenth-century copies — or restorations — simply by the condition of the stone and the degree of weathering or decay. This test, though, is by no means infallible. Depending on the quality of the stone and the cleanliness of the atmosphere, some medieval stonework is almost as sharp as when it was first cut, while some Victorian work has weathered very badly. Victorian work can sometimes be distinguished by its more regular, even mechanical character, but in many cases, especially when the work has been done carefully and well, it can be very difficult to distinguish medieval from Victorian work, although medieval figure sculpture is often more robust — even grotesque — in design, than most Victorian

171

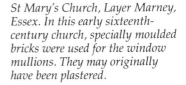

St Mary's Church, Layer Marney, Essex. In this early sixteenth-century church, specially moulded bricks were used for the window mullions. They may originally have been plastered.

work. It is always worth examining the jambs and surrounds of external doorways for traces of mass-dials (primitive sundials cut to indicate the time for Mass). These are inscribed circles with central holes, for the gnomon, and are practically certain to indicate that the stonework has not been renewed. Stone consecration crosses may also survive in external walls, but these were often simply painted on the old external plaster which may since have been stripped.

So far we have been considering stone-built churches, but brickwork can also help with dating. The first post-Roman brickwork in England dates from the thirteenth century onwards, when it began to be used in East Anglia and Essex — areas lacking good building stone. In many churches in these areas brick, as we have seen, was used for the general walling, with stone reserved for details, although sometimes specially moulded bricks were used in window tracery. Most of this early brickwork was probably plastered but, as happened with rubble stonework, it has often been stripped. Early bricks are generally quite easy to recognise, being thinner and rather rougher than modern bricks, and not always laid to any regular bond.

Later, the use of brick spread across the country, becoming quite general by the eighteenth century. These Georgian bricks were similar in size to modern ones but, being handmade, they often show some variation of colour and texture. In the nineteenth century machine-made bricks of more uniform colour and texture became available in all parts of the country, and their use in Gothic-style churches is an almost certain indication of Victorian or later date.

It is not usual to find date stones on churches before the eighteenth century, but occasionally they were built into the walls, particularly in the seventeenth and eighteenth centuries to indicate the date of repairs or alterations. They often bear the initials of the incumbent and churchwardens. Dates are also sometimes shown on sundials built into the south wall, but these, of course, do not always refer to the date of the church itself.

Turning from the walls to the roof, this is rather less reliable as a guide to dating the building, since the roof-covering of an old church will probably have been relaid several times, often with a change of material. In early medieval times, as we have seen, most churches were thatched, and a few examples have survived, particularly in Norfolk and Suffolk. Stone slates and, indeed, true slates, were probably used from an early date in areas near their quarries. Tiles were first introduced into Kent and East Anglia at the end of the Middle Ages, and their use spread to most other areas by the eighteenth century. By the nineteenth century, tiles and slates were being used all over the country. It will often be found that a

LEFT *A mass-dial on one of the door jambs of St Mary's Church, Bibury, Glos. This can be taken as evidence of original, unrestored, stonework. Such dials, scratched on the masonry, are commonly found near the entrances to medieval churches.* RIGHT *SS Peter and Paul's Church, Pickering, North Yorks, an eighteenth-century sundial fixed to a fourteenth-century porch.*

typical nineteenth-century tiled or slated roof, with ornamental ridges and iron gutters, covers a much older building. Lead was the most usual material for the later medieval low-pitched roofs, especially on the greater churches and the richer parish churches.

In an earlier chapter I described some of the local variations in the style of medieval churches. These local characteristics were not always appreciated by the Victorian church builders and restorers, who were often aiming at their idealised version of the style of the late thirteenth and early fourteenth centuries. This was sometimes combined with the introduction of elements from foreign Gothic work of the same period, perhaps influenced by the writings of Ruskin. Complete churches, or features in older churches in a definitely non-local idiom, are likely to be nineteenth-century work.

Another clue to Victorian building or restoration may be found in the individual styles of particular architects. While the leading church architects of the period carried out work — both new churches and restorations — in many parts of the country, others worked mainly in their own areas, and it is sometimes possible to recognise their styles and individual design features in local churches. These may be seen in such things as window tracery, coping and parapet details, or even the ornamental ironwork on doors. As we have seen, some architects, especially those supporting the views of William Morris and the Society for the Protection of Ancient Buildings, adopted a very conservative approach to restoration, keeping as much old work as possible, and carrying out very sensitive repairs and renewals. Others renewed more drastically, but always replacing old work by exact replicas. Others again tried to put the church back to its presumed state in the early fourteenth century, while another group unashamedly imposed their own ideas - not necessarily conforming to any medieval style.

It should by now be clear that we can learn a great deal about the age and architectural history of a church by walking round the outside. However, the fact that the exterior has been subject to far more weathering and deterioration than the interior means that it is more likely to have been subject to repair and renewal, sometimes amounting to a complete external refacing. A church on an old site which appears from the outside to be entirely of the nineteenth century can still present some surprises when we go inside.

St Mary's Roman Catholic Church, Hastings, Sussex, built in 1882 by Basil Champneys, using the local flint, is Gothic in style. The gabled buttress tops, level with the coping, the high windows in the apse, and the design of the stair turret would all make one question a medieval date for the building. It is the work of a late Victorian architect with a style of his own.

12

Looking at a Church, the interior

Although the exterior of a church can tell us much about its history, the interior can sometimes be a surprise. Even if the exterior has been drastically restored, because of exposure to the weather and atmospheric pollution, the interior may retain more original features. Going into an old church we may have to step *down* into the nave, because the ground level outside has been raised by successive burials. This will rarely be the case with a nineteenth- or twentieth-century church, where we are more likely to be stepping *up* as we go in.

In an old church, the principal entrance is likely to be on the south side, but there will often be a north door opposite this, perhaps now blocked up. As we have seen, a Norman doorway may be in its original position, but it is quite likely to have been reset in a later aisle wall. It does, though, indicate a Norman, if not earlier, *origin* for the building.

Once inside the church it is interesting to try to work out its development, starting with the plan form. Does the church appear to be all of one build, or has it developed over the centuries? If the architectural style is uniform throughout the building, apart perhaps from some later inserted windows, then it is likely that the present plan represents the church as first built. It is far more likely, though, that there has been a story of continuous change and development — usually a progressive enlargement — of the church, from a simple, probably unaisled, or possibly cruciform building.

The different styles of, for instance, window tracery, arcade details, ornamental mouldings, described in an earlier chapter, will help to date the various parts of the church, but we shall need to interpret these to work out just how it has been changed. In an aisled church, are the two arcades of matching design? It will often be found that one, usually the

St Mary's Church, East Brent, Somerset. The fifteenth-century door leads into a church of the same period, with some contemporary seating. It also contains a seventeenth-century west gallery, made up of parts of the rood screen, and (out of the picture) an enriched plaster ceiling dated 1637.

north arcade, for reasons described earlier, is older. Look too for evidence of blocked openings in the upper parts of the arcade walls, indicating that these were the *external* walls of the original church. The arcades themselves may not be uniform in style. A church may have been extended westwards, and in this case the western bays of the arcade will be in a later style.

Is there a clerestory? And if so, are its windows of similar style to that of the arcades? Often they will be found to be later, and further proof that the walls have been raised to accommodate a clerestory may be shown by the outline of an earlier, lower, roof against a west tower or the wall over the chancel arch. Are the aisle windows of the same style as the arcades? If, as is often the case, they are *later* in date this could indicate either straightforward replacement of the windows, or a later widening of the aisle. Evidence of the latter is more likely to be shown *externally*, by straight joints. Internally these will be hidden under later plaster unless this has been stripped by over-zealous Victorian restorers.

Still looking at the aisles and arcades, there may be some irregularity of

St Mary and All Saints' Church, Willoughby-on-the-Wolds, Notts. The outline of an older, lower but steeper roof can be seen on the east wall, above the Royal Arms. The arcade walls have been raised to form a clerestory.

LEFT *SS Mary and Helen's Church, Elstow, Beds. This church, perhaps best known for its connection with John Bunyan, was formerly monastic. The Norman nave was extended to the west in the thirteenth century. One of these later arches shows dogtooth ornament. Note also the Royal Arms of 1773.*

design at the east end of the nave, adjoining the chancel. This could indicate the incorporation of earlier transepts into the aisles, and even, in some cases, the removal of a central tower.

Enlargement of older churches was less common after the Reformation. Additional seating, when required, was more usually provided by inserting galleries, but occasionally an aisle was added. Such additions were generally in a Classical style, with round arches, but sometimes a Gothic design was adopted. This eighteenth-century Gothic varied considerably in its authenticity. Some examples are quite difficult to distinguish from genuine medieval work, while others are obviously of a later date, sometimes incorporating some Classical details.

Victorian additions to medieval churches are much more common, reflecting the increased population of the time. Again, some Victorian work follows medieval examples very closely, and can only be identified by its sharper and more mechanical details and, perhaps, the use of non-local materials. Some Victorian architects even introduced polished granite in areas far from its source. In other cases the design is less

179

Holy Trinity Church, Millom, Cumbria. The church is of Norman origin, but this unusual oval window was inserted in the fourteenth century. The roof is of tie and collar-beam construction, with arched braces to alternate trusses, but no ridge piece, the common rafters being coupled together at the top.

180

This paired thirteenth-century window was originally shuttered, as can be seen by the rebate in the stonework at Holy Saviour's Church, Puxton, Avon.

orthodox, and some of the later Victorian architects had, as we have seen, a distinctive style of their own. We must, though, remember the Victorian inclination to imitate the work of the late thirteenth and early fourteenth centuries, often regardless of the original style of the building. By the later nineteenth century, under the influence of the Arts and Crafts movement, any additions to churches were generally in a freer interpretation of Gothic, as it was now considered wrong to imitate past styles or to attempt to falsify the history of the building. In our own time, old churches have sometimes been enlarged in a frankly modern style, with varying degrees of success.

In the later Middle Ages the earlier small Norman and lancet windows were often replaced by larger traceried windows to take stained glass. In a thirteenth-century chancel — often a rebuilding and lengthening of a small Norman one — the original east window, perhaps a triple lancet, will often have been replaced by a larger window of the fourteenth or fifteenth century. Sometimes, though, the evidence of the old window can still be seen, perhaps the remains of a rere-arch with detached jamb shafts. In the north and south chancel walls the old lancets may well have been left.

Still in the chancel, it is worth looking at its size in relation to that of the rest of the church. We have seen that the chancels of Norman churches were often rebuilt on a larger scale in the thirteenth century to

181

accommodate the more elaborate ceremonial. If, though, the chancel seems exceptionally large, the church may originally have been collegiate, or even monastic, as well as serving as the parish church. These chancels were sometimes demolished after the Dissolution. A good example of a collegiate chancel remains at Cobham Church, Kent, now perhaps most famous for its collection of memorial brasses.

Blocked arches in external walls will tell us of demolished parts of the building — aisles or chapels. This, as we have seen, often indicates a decline in the population or the prosperity of the parish — the people could no longer afford to maintain the whole building. Chapels may have been demolished after the Reformation. Where we find that a whole chancel has been demolished, the blocked chancel arch now in the east wall of the church, it is likely that the church was monastic or collegiate, the chancel having been demolished at the Dissolution, leaving only the parochial nave. This may be seen at Carisbrooke in the Isle of Wight.

Before the Reformation most parish churches contained several chapels, each with its own altar. Some of these chapels were separate structures, built out from the main body of the church, but many were simply screened off from the aisles. Each altar would have had a piscina (a small arched recess containing a drain for washing the communion vessels) and many of these have survived, although the altars have long since gone. This can help us to reconstruct the medieval internal arrangement of the church. Squints, or openings cut through the walls on each side of the chancel arch, may also provide evidence of further altars in the aisles. Although there is no firm evidence of their original purpose, they could have enabled the priest celebrating Mass at a side altar to see the celebration at the high altar, and perhaps synchronise the actual consecration in the two services.

Another feature of medieval chancels that has given rise to much speculation is the low window sometimes found near the chancel arch, usually on the south side, near the site of the original clergy stall. These windows have sometimes been called 'leper windows', but since at that time lepers would probably not have been allowed in the churchyard this explanation is unlikely to be true. They may have been used to enable a handbell to be rung outside the church at the time of the consecration at Mass, possible evidence for this being provided by the fact that many of them appear to have been rebated for shutters while all other windows in the chancel were glazed. On the other hand, the window may simply have been provided to give more light to the clergy stall.

Also in the chancel we may find sedilia (seats for the clergy) recessed into the wall, again on the south side. Often there are three seats together, either for the priest and two servers or for three priests at High Mass.

RIGHT *Fourteenth-century sedilia, with ogee arches to the canopies, at St Laurence's Church, Whitwell, Derbys.*

BELOW *St Michael's Church, Laxton, Notts, the fourteenth-century sedilia and double piscina. These features can often give a clue to the original floor levels. The village is noted for its surviving open field system.*

ABOVE *St Peter's Church, Sibthorpe, Notts. A detail from the fourteenth-century Easter Sepulchre, showing the risen Christ between angels with censers.* RIGHT *All Saints' Church, Hawton, Notts. A detail from the famous fourteenth-century Easter Sepulchre, showing the sleeping soldiers.*

Their position can give a clue to the original floor level in the sanctuary, which was sometimes raised in Victorian times to enable the altar to be seen more clearly from the nave. A similar, single recess in the north wall of the chancel may have been an Easter Sepulchre, where the consecrated host was kept from Good Friday until Easter Day. Many of these Easter Sepulchres were destroyed or mutilated at the time of the Reformation, but a particularly fine example still exists at Hawton, Nottinghamshire, and there are others in the same area.

Most medieval churches, except where the walls were faced with fine ashlar, were originally plastered internally. Surviving medieval plaster can usually be identified by the fact that it is quite thin, and follows the contours of the rubble wall face, and is therefore slightly irregular in profile. It also finished flush with the dressed stones of the door and window jambs. This plaster was usually limewashed and decorated, either with formal designs, or pictorial scenes. These decorations were periodically renewed during the Middle Ages, but were generally whitened over after the Reformation. In more recent times some have been uncovered, and it is sometimes possible to see the remains of several layers of paintings.

In the seventeenth and eighteenth centuries a rather thicker plaster,

SS Mary and Andrew's Church, Horsham St Faith, Norfolk. Painting of a saint, on the rood screen. These paintings are dated 1528.

often mixed with hair, was used, and when earlier churches were replastered at this time the plaster, sometimes applied *over* the medieval plaster, was often carried over the stone quoins to the door and window openings, and even at times over moulded work. This later plaster was frequently stripped by the Victorians, sometimes revealing the earlier plaster below, but all too often destroying it in the mistaken idea that it was also post-medieval and of no value. They then usually left the internal rubble walling exposed, but if they replastered it was generally in rather a hard mix with a level surface, unlike the soft medieval plaster. It was sometimes finished flush with the stone quoins but often, being thicker than the medieval plaster, was finished proud of them. Occasionally we find nineteenth-century plaster applied *over* medieval plaster, and it has sometimes been possible to remove the later layer, perhaps exposing traces of early wall painting.

From the walls, look up at the roof. In a parish church this is likely to be of timber, although some Norman chancels were vaulted. Cathedral, collegiate and monastic churches were more likely to have stone vaulted roofs throughout the building. We have looked at the development of medieval roof design, from the early, simple, rather steeply pitched roofs to the more elaborate roofs of the later Middle Ages, but timber roofs, being less durable than stone, were often renewed more than once in the history of a church. In the seventeenth and eighteenth centuries this renewal was generally carried out in a strictly utilitarian manner, with little respect for the original design. Some roofs of this period were of simple king-post or queen-post form, and we may well find the date, and the names or initials of the churchwardens, cut on one of the roof beams. In other cases the medieval roof was hidden by a plaster ceiling, which may be either flat or following the line of the original roof. These ceilings were often removed by Victorian restorers, the only remaining evidence for such a ceiling being the nail holes for the laths, seen on the rafters. The Victorians also, though, removed medieval plastered panels from barrel or waggon roofs. These originally plastered roofs can generally be identified not only by the nail holes in the rafters but also by the moulded ribs which had separated the panels.

Many church roofs were renewed, or substantially restored, during the nineteenth century, and as with all Victorian restoration the degree and nature of the repair varies considerably. In some cases we will find that all possible original work has been kept, the repairs being as unobtrusive as possible, and therefore difficult to recognise from floor level. Often, though, the roof was completely renewed, generally in pine rather than

St Illtud's Church, Llantwit Major, South Glamorgan, Wales. The underside of this arch-braced roof, with its carved bosses, may originally have been plastered.

The painted roof of this chapel at Rhug, mid Wales is dated 1637, but it is still of medieval design, perhaps an example of architectural time-lag.

oak, and not necessarily following the original design. Where a steeply pitched early medieval roof had been replaced by one of flatter pitch in, say, the fifteenth century, the Victorians would often restore the original roof line. Evidence of these successive changes can sometimes be traced on the east and west walls.

The floor of an old church can tell us something of its history. In the early Middle Ages, small churches may well have had floors of beaten earth, or lime-ash, but those of larger churches would have been paved in stone or, from the thirteenth century onwards, with tiles. By the later Middle Ages even the small churches had stone floors, with perhaps some ornamental tiling in the chancel. Unless the chancel floor was laid over a crypt, or followed the slope of the ground, it was generally level with that of the nave, with perhaps one or two steps in the sanctuary. As we have seen, the Victorians often inserted extra steps in the chancel, and evidence of the original levels may be provided by the heights of the piscina and sedilia. Old stone floors may incorporate graveslabs and brasses, but these may not be in their original positions — they were often moved by later restorers. In the eighteenth century, stone paving was usual in churches, and this was sometimes laid in formal patterns, incorporating small squares of slate or a darker stone.

Timber flooring under the pews was rare before the nineteenth century, when it was introduced to provide a warmer finish. At this time many churches were re-floored, not only to raise the levels in the chancel but also under the pews in the nave and aisles, generally in conjunction with re-pewing and perhaps the installation of central heating, with pipes laid in floor ducts. The Victorians generally favoured tiled flooring, except under the pews, and many copies of medieval ornamental tiles were made at this time.

We have looked at the development of window tracery, and seen how it can help in dating, always remembering that windows were often enlarged and renewed. The actual glazing may also be worthy of study. Most windows in medieval churches were filled with stained glass, wired for support to iron saddle bars and stancheons, known as *ferramenta*. For reasons we have seen, it is comparatively rare to find medieval windows with their glass intact. Far more often, fragments of old glass have been

Thirteenth-century floor tiles at Strata Florida Abbey, Dyfed, Wales. These are from an abbey, but many parish churches had tiled floors, especially in the chancel, by the fourteenth century.

LEFT *St Paul's Church, Morton, Gainsborough, Lincs, stained glass window by Burne-Jones, showing the stoning of Stephen.*

St Michael's Church, Halam, Notts. Fifteenth-century stained glass, showing Adam delving. The treatment of a biblical subject should be compared with that in the nineteenth-century glass opposite. Note also the architectural framework to the figure.

rescued from various windows and been refixed. Exceptions occur in places such as York, where much of the medieval glass in the Minster and the parish churches survived the Civil War because of the influence of General Fairfax. The church at Fairford, Gloucestershire, also retains all its late medieval glass, although this has been taken out and refixed more than once.

In the seventeenth and eighteenth centuries most windows were reglazed with crown glass in rectangular leaded panes. This can be recognised by its slightly irregular surface. In the nineteenth century much new stained glass was inserted, as well as tinted and textured glass, generally in diamond panes.

We shall be looking at furnishings and fittings in the next chapter, but it is worthwhile looking for evidence of *vanished* fittings. The remains of the stairs, with the upper and lower doorways, to the rood loft, may often be found near the chancel arch. At the west end, a window at an unusual level may have lit a former west gallery. Marks on old plaster, and even notches cut in arcade columns, may provide evidence of former box pews, or a high pulpit removed in a later restoration.

Finally, there may be, somewhere in the church, old paintings or prints showing it before restoration. Even allowing for some artistic licence which may make us wonder whether the church was as 'ruinous' as it was depicted, these can give us an insight into the changes of the last hundred years.

St Mary's Church, Redgrave, Suffolk. The early eighteenth-century memorial by Green of Camberwell. By the eighteenth century, figures on monuments were generally depicted in life-like poses combined with allegorical figures, such as Justice, which appears on the left.

13

Furnishings and Fittings

The furnishings in a church can be as interesting as the building itself, although more often than not they are not contemporary with the fabric. Far more often, the furnishings are later than the building, but occasionally they may be earlier, having been re-used, either from an older church on the site or, increasingly today as churches are made redundant, from a completely different building. We are more likely to find an eighteenth- or nineteenth-century church complete with its original fittings than a medieval church, but churches have at all times been subject to changes in fashion, and in forms of worship, which have had more effect on the fittings than on the fabric itself. Let us look, then, at the various fittings to be found in a church, and see what they can tell us about its history, starting in the chancel.

Altars and Communion Tables

In pre-Reformation times the altar was almost always of stone, being either a solid structure, or with a top — the mensa — carried on stone piers. The mensa always had five inscribed crosses, one in each corner and one in the centre. After the Reformation, orders were given for these stone altars to be removed and replaced with movable wooden tables, and very few have survived intact. Sometimes the mensa was set in the floor as a paving slab, and can be recognised by the five crosses. One was used as a fireplace lintel in a cottage at Piddletrenthide, Dorset. In the nineteenth and twentieth centuries some of these mensae have been restored, on new wood or stone supports.

The earliest wooden communion tables generally consisted of a board supported on trestles, and again very few have survived. In the later sixteenth and seventeenth centuries the usual form resembled the normal domestic tables of the time, and a large number have survived, the most typical design perhaps being the Elizabethan and Jacobean tables with bulbous turned legs. They are generally rather shorter than the medieval

St Bartholomew's Church, Corton, Dorset. The medieval altar stone in this little church survived the Reformation and has now been refixed, on new stone supports.

stone altars, probably to make it more convenient for the communicants to kneel all round them. Some of these surviving tables are no longer used for their original purpose and may be found as book tables at the back of the church, or in the vestry.

Stone altars were occasionally used in the eighteenth century in spite of their being, strictly speaking, illegal. An interesting example, the front carved to represent drapery, can be seen at Milton Abbey Church, Dorset. In the nineteenth century stone altars became rather more common, particularly in the Catholic wing of the Church, but they were far more often of wood, either of table form or with solid panelled fronts. The canons of the Church required the altar to be covered with a frontal during the communion service, but bare unvested altars became more common in the nineteenth century. Medieval frontals were generally of the flat type usual today, but in the seventeenth and eighteenth centuries the draped frontal, covering the altar on all sides, was more common. In recent years there has been a trend to move the altar from the chancel into the nave, to encourage greater participation in the service by the congregation — a return to the practice of the sixteenth-century reformers.

Altar ornaments, the cross and candlesticks, are likely to be nineteenth-century or later. Eighteenth-century candlesticks found are quite likely to have been brought from elsewhere, often from Continental sources.

Reredoses, Altarpieces and Altar Rails

In medieval times these might be of stone, alabaster or wood, often consisting of a series of carved figures in niches, and generally coloured. They were normally about equal in height to that of the altar itself, finishing just below the sill of the east window, but occasionally the reredos covered the whole east wall. Many were destroyed at the Reformation, and others mutilated by the destruction of the figures. These were sometimes restored in the nineteenth and twentieth centuries. Medieval illuminated manuscripts and other contemporary sources often

194

show the altar flanked by curtains at each end, at right angles to the east wall, sometimes carried on brackets and sometimes with vertical posts in line with the front of the altar, forming what has become known as the 'English altar'. There might also be a tester or canopy suspended above the altar. This form was often revived in the early twentieth century.

In the seventeenth and eighteenth centuries the altarpiece often consisted of wood panelling, sometimes of Classical design, with columns supporting a pediment and inscribed with the Creed, the Lord's Prayer and the Ten Commandments. These were sometimes further enriched by painted figures of Moses and Aaron, and surmounted by a sacred monogram surrounded by the sun's rays. Particularly fine examples of these can be seen in some of Wren's City of London churches. In the nineteenth century this type of altarpiece was regarded as 'pagan' and many were removed.

Nineteenth-century altarpieces take many different forms. These may be of wood, stone or marble, sometimes with carved figures in medieval style. Others were formed of ornamental tiling or mosaic. There was often a shelf, or gradine, at the base, to take the altar ornaments. In recent times some of these Victorian altarpieces have been covered by curtains, being considered over-ornate, but with a further change of taste some of them are now being uncovered again. As we have seen, in the early years of the present century the English Altar was revived, under the influence of the Arts and Crafts movement, the supporting posts (or riddels) often being capped by carved angels carrying candles.

The Early Christian ciborium or baldachino, a solid canopy over the altar, mounted on free-standing columns, was not common in England, but examples can be found in nineteenth- and twentieth-century churches.

There is no evidence for the use of altar rails before the Reformation. At this time the majority of people received Communion infrequently, and in one kind only. Rails appear to have been introduced in the early seventeenth century, as part of Archbishop Laud's reforms, when the altar was moved back to its pre-Reformation position against the east wall of the chancel. These rails were designed to protect the altar from irreverent use, including keeping dogs away from it, and the examples of this period usually extended straight across the chancel for its full width, with gates in the centre. The uprights or balusters were generally turned, and fixed closely together. Sometimes the newels, with spherical or shaped tops, extended above the rail itself.

In the Commonwealth period, when the Elizabethan chancel arrangements were restored, and the altar brought out into the centre of the chancel, the rails were abandoned, and most were destroyed, although examples may still be found.

St Katharine's Church, Chislehampton, Oxon. This church of c.1763 retains most of its eighteenth-century fittings, including the fine panelled altarpiece with the Creed, Lord's Prayer, and Commandments. The altar rails and box pews are contemporary with the church, but the pulpit, of the early seventeenth century, predates it, as indicated by the Jacobean carving.

After the Restoration of King Charles II the altar was again moved back against the east wall, and enclosed by rails. At this period, though, these were generally 'returned' at each end of the altar, enclosing it on three sides. The rails were generally of timber, with turned balusters, and this form continued through the eighteenth century.

In the nineteenth century rails were often of metal – brass, wrought or cast iron, and the uprights were more widely spaced. In place of the central gates there was often a hinged or sliding bar to give access to the altar. In the early twentieth century, and corresponding with the fashion for the 'English' altar, rails were sometimes replaced by movable wooden kneeling desks. Both forms are found in modern churches.

Aumbries and Tabernacles

Reservation of the Sacrament (the keeping of the consecrated bread and

196

wine) in medieval times was generally in a pyx, hanging in front of the altar. These have rarely survived, but a few late nineteenth-century examples may be found, generally of silver and looking rather like a solid hanging lamp. When reservation, banned at the Reformation, was again permitted in the late nineteenth century it was, and often still is, in an 'aumbry' or cupboard at one side of the altar. Medieval aumbries, though, were more often used simply as safes or cupboards. The tabernacle or box, on the altar itself, or the gradine, a Continental introduction, is found in some churches and is always of nineteenth- or twentieth-century date.

Chancel Seating

We have seen in an earlier chapter how seats were often provided in the Middle Ages for the clergy officiating at Mass, in the form of recessed stone benches, generally canopied, known as sedilia. Additional clergy stalls were also constructed of timber, especially in collegiate and larger churches, and these, although more susceptible to damage or loss, have sometimes survived. Medieval stalls, generally only of one row each side in parish churches, were sited along the western parts of the side walls, and were often returned against the screen, facing east. They generally had carved ends, and panelled fronts to the kneeling desks, and sometimes the tip-up seats, or misericords, more often found in cathedral

Tansor Church, Northants. These clergy stalls, with carved misericords, were formerly in Fotheringhay Church, where the collegiate choir was demolished after the Reformation.

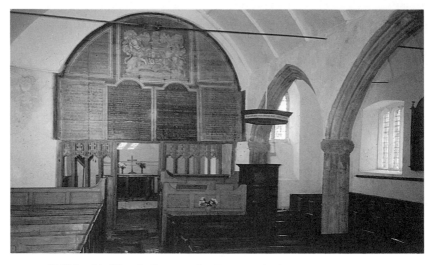

ABOVE *St Petrock's Church, Parracombe, Devon. The late medieval screen retains its tympanum, now painted with the Royal Arms, Creed, Lord's Prayer and Commandments.* RIGHT *All Saints' Church, Bolton, Cumbria. This eighteenth-century early Gothic Revival screen fills the upper part of the chancel arch. Screens of this period are rare. Above it is a Royal Arms of Victoria. Note also the font, with its cover, dated 1687.*

and monastic churches. The undersides of these misericord seats were usually enriched with carvings, often of a secular, indeed humorous, character.

After the Reformation the congregation moved into the chancel for the second part of the Communion service, and seats were sometimes provided for them in addition to, or perhaps replacing, the medieval clergy stalls. These seats were sometimes carried across the east wall, thus surrounding the altar, which had been brought into the centre of the chancel, on three sides. These sixteenth- and early seventeenth-century communicants' seats sometimes survive, adapted as choirstalls in the nineteenth century, but they have generally been removed from the east wall. Deerhurst Church, Gloucestershire, is one of the few where this arrangement can still be seen. These seats can be recognised by their typical Elizabethan or Jacobean design.

In the nineteenth century it became usual for the choir to be seated in the chancel, and stalls had to be provided for them, often two or three rows on each side. Nineteenth-century choirstalls may be of oak or pine, sometimes of Gothic design, and occasionally incorporating older woodwork from dismantled medieval or later seating. These choirstalls, inserted in churches which were never designed to hold them, can give the chancel rather a crowded appearance and in recent years there has been a move to take them out of the chancel into, say, the eastern part of the nave or an aisle.

198

Occasionally we may find individual chairs in the chancel, often good examples of seventeenth or eighteenth century furniture. These may have been made for the church, but are quite likely to have been brought from elsewhere. In the nineteenth century a good deal of foreign woodwork, much of it Flemish in origin, was introduced into churches by travelling clergymen or squires.

Screens

Medieval churches probably all had a screen between the nave and the chancel, whether or not there was a structural chancel arch, surmounted by the rood loft. Often the space between the top of the loft and the chancel arch, or the underside of the roof if there was no arch, was filled in with a lath and plaster partition, known as a tympanum, originally painted with a representation of the Last Judgement. After the Reformation this was normally painted over with the Royal Arms, or with biblical texts. Most tympana were removed by Victorian restorers who believed them to be post-medieval. A fine example survives at Lockington, Leicestershire, and there are others in the old church at Parracombe, Devon, and Warminghurst, Sussex — both these latter churches being vested in the Redundant Churches Fund.

St Mary and All Saints' Church, Dunsfold, Surrey. The curiously shaped pews are believed to date from the thirteenth century. If so, they are contemporary with the church. It is rare to find seating for the congregation of this early date.

The early chancel screens were quite simple in design, and there is a good one at Higham, Kent, but later medieval screens were often elaborate and there were distinct regional variations in their style. Screens also separated the chancel from its aisles, and served to partition off side chapels and altars. Some screens were removed at the Reformation, others during the seventeenth and eighteenth centuries, and a few even as late as the nineteenth century. Sometimes we find the upper part of the chancel screen has been cut away, leaving only the solid lower panels. The loft was occasionally adapted and refixed to form a west gallery, where it may be recognised by its medieval details.

Although most medieval screens were of wood, stone screens are occasionally found, as at Stebbing, Essex, and Cerne Abbas, Dorset. In both these cases the lofts have gone, and these may have been of wood. As we have seen, the Elizabethan canons required the retention of the chancel screen, and post-Reformation examples are sometimes found, even as late as the eighteenth century, although by then they were far less common. Good examples of seventeenth-century screens may be seen at Croscombe, Somerset, and Staunton Harold, in Leicestershire. There are fine eighteenth-century screens, of wrought iron, in Derby Cathedral — formerly a parish church.

200

Many new screens were installed in the nineteenth century, occasionally with lofts and most often of Gothic design. They can generally be distinguished from medieval examples by the more mechanical nature of their carving. Iron screens were also popular at this time, and sometimes a low screen wall was preferred, as causing less visual division between the nave and the chancel.

Nave Seating

The earliest form of seating for the congregation was in the form of solid stone benches round the walls. By the fourteenth century some wooden seating was sometimes provided, in the form of very plain benches, often without backs. In the fifteenth century fixed seating was becoming more common, but the aisles or gangways between the blocks of seating were quite wide. The bench ends were often richly carved, sometimes with heraldic or non-religious subjects. Occasionally, seating in the aisles was planned to face inwards, as can be seen at the church of Walpole Saint Peter, Norfolk.

In the seventeenth and eighteenth centuries, fixed seating was universal, either in the form of benches, often with enclosing doors at

St Michael's Church, Stragglethorpe, Lincs. Two-decker pulpit and box pews, of the eighteenth century.

each end, or as high box pews. The early examples are generally of oak, panelled, and sometimes with strapwork or other typical decoration of the period. These pews were often paid for by the families using them, and in some churches, such as that at West Chiltington, Sussex, the names of the families were painted on the pews. The pews of the wealthier families were often comfortably fitted out, sometimes with canopies, and even fireplaces. Particularly fine examples can be seen at the Ryecote Chapel, Oxfordshire (see page 104).

Although during the seventeenth and eighteenth centuries the choir were normally seated in a west gallery, they were sometimes placed at the west end of the nave, generally on a raised platform. These raised seats have sometimes survived, although they may no longer be used by the choir.

In the mid to late nineteenth century many of the box pews were removed and replaced by benches inspired by those of the Middle Ages, and the system of pew rents was eventually abolished. Sometimes material from the old box pews was incorporated in their replacements. In other cases, material from medieval seating was rescued and re-used, particularly the carved bench ends. Victorian seating may be of oak or

LEFT *St Anthony's Church, Cartmel Fell, Cumbria. The late seventeenth-century screened pew, and three-decker pulpit, seen through a medieval screen.*

BELOW LEFT *St Mary's Church, Bishops Lydeard, Somerset, a fifteenth-century bench end showing a windmill.* BELOW RIGHT *Early sixteenth-century bench end, showing a helmeted warrior, at SS Peter and Paul's Church, Lingfield, Surrey. This church, formerly collegiate, contains a fine collection of monuments to the Cobham family.*

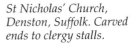
*St Nicholas' Church,
Denston, Suffolk. Carved
ends to clergy stalls.*

pine, and varies considerably in design, some examples being very plain, with open backs, while others are quite ornate. The main difference between medieval and Victorian seating is perhaps in their density, the aisles or gangways between the blocks of seating being far narrower in most Victorian examples, giving the church rather a crowded appearance compared with the effect of medieval seating. In more recent times there has been a trend to remove some of the Victorian seats, creating more space and, perhaps, reflecting the smaller congregations of today.

Fonts

In Saxon and Norman times baptism of infants by immersion was the normal practice, and fonts were therefore quite large. Most Norman fonts were either tub-shaped, or based on a square bowl on a circular stem, sometimes with additional columns. Lead fonts of Norman and early medieval date are occasionally found, with cast decoration. In the later Middle Ages when immersion was less common, fonts became smaller, and were generally octagonal in plan. The sides of the bowl were often decorated, either with traceried panels reflecting the current style of window tracery (an aid to dating), or with carved ornament, the Seven Sacraments plus the Crucifixion being popular subjects.

Originally the font was generally placed near the principal entrance to the church, but they have often been moved, reflecting changes in baptismal practice. Fonts were also moved from an earlier church to a later one on the site. It is not uncommon to find, say, a Norman font in a church which appears completely late medieval.

Some five hundred years of baptism separate the thirteenth-century font at SS Peter and Paul's Church at Knapton, Norfolk, from its handsome cover of 1704. This is a fine example of how disparate styles can combine in church furnishings, just as in the fabric of the building.

205

Furnishings and Fittings

Because the baptismal water was blessed at Easter and kept for the whole year in the font, there was a fear that it might be stolen for witchcraft or black magic purposes, and all fonts had to be provided with locked covers. At first these were simple wooden lids, but by the late Middle Ages font covers were often very elaborate steeple-like constructions, which had to be raised and lowered by pulleys and counterweights.

By the eighteenth century fonts had become much smaller, the typical form being a shallow bowl on a turned baluster support, the 'vase' font. At this time marble was a common material for fonts. For a time it became popular to move the font to the east end of the church, often close to the altar, but this arrangement was generally reversed by the Victorians.

During the eighteenth, and even at times in the nineteenth century, older fonts were sometimes discarded, being used as garden ornaments or even as farm feeding troughs. These old fonts have sometimes been recovered and restored to the church in recent times, so that we may find a church with two fonts — the original one and its later replacement. In the nineteenth century new fonts generally followed the typical later medieval form, although other designs are sometimes found, including one in the form of a marble angel holding a shell. Although a position

St Margaret's Church, Burnham Norton, Norfolk. The fifteenth-century pulpit has paintings of the four Latin Doctors of the Church.

The pulpit, of 1775, at SS Peter and Paul's Church, Trottiscliffe, Kent, was originally in Westminster Abbey, and was brought to Trottiscliffe in 1824 by the Dean and Chapter, patrons of the Church.

near the west end, or near the principal doorway, was generally favoured, there was another fashion during the nineteenth century for setting the font in a separate baptistry, sometimes apsidal, built out from a side wall of the church. In recent times fonts have been re-sited yet again, sometimes near the east end, as baptism within the main service, rather than a semi-private function, has become more popular.

Pulpits

Pulpits were rare in parish churches before the fifteenth century, but from this period onwards, as preaching became more important, they were more common. Medieval pulpits are found made of both wood and stone, often of a 'wine glass' form, on quite a slender stem, and sometimes with traceried sides, the tracery echoing that found in contemporary windows.

After the Reformation, pulpits were installed in all churches. They were now generally of wood, the panelling often showing the typical strapwork patterns of the late sixteenth and early seventeenth centuries, and they sometimes had sounding boards. It soon became common to combine the pulpit with the reading pew and sometimes the clerk's desk, to form a two- or three-decker. The pulpit was at the highest level, necessary to enable the preacher's voice to reach the congregation when box pews and galleries were common.

In the eighteenth century, in medieval churches with rather a long plan form, the pulpit was sometimes sited part-way down the nave, on one side, the seats east of it being made to face *west* towards the pulpit and away from the altar, which had become less significant as Communion services were held less often. Pulpits at this time were often fitted with hour-glasses, to time the sermon, and even when the glass itself has gone its supporting brackets may remain.

In the nineteenth century, with the change of emphasis from preaching to the sacraments, the pulpit became less dominant. Many of the old three-deckers were removed, and others altered and reduced in height, coinciding with the removal of the box pews and galleries. Pulpits which had been fixed partway down the nave were generally refixed nearer the chancel. Since it had become more usual for the priest to conduct the service from a stall in the chancel, the reading pew became redundant, and the parish clerk lost his old function of leading the congregational singing. Victorian pulpits are generally of Gothic, or even Norman, design, although there was no historical precedent for the latter style. They may be of wood, stone, marble or alabaster, sometimes decorated with mosaics. Sounding boards became less common, and some were removed from older pulpits, occasionally being re-used as table tops.

It is fair to say that in the great majority of parish churches the box pews and three-decker pulpits of the seventeenth and eighteenth centuries were removed by the Victorians to suit the new, or revived, ways of worship. Where they have survived it is generally for one of two reasons: either the population had moved and a new church had been built for them, leaving the old church largely unused, except perhaps for funerals if the old churchyard was still in use; or there was a succession of conservative squires, or rectors, or both, who preferred the old ways, enabling the pre-Tractarian arrangements to survive long enough to be considered worthy of preservation on historical grounds. Occasionally we find a church, largely refurnished, but retaining one or two family pews, the families concerned having resisted their removal.

Galleries

From the later sixteenth until the nineteenth century the west gallery was the most usual place for the church choir and, later, the organ. Sometimes the material from a medieval rood loft was used to make a gallery front — these can be recognised by their medieval detail. Generally, gallery fronts are of panelled wood, sometimes with the typical mouldings or ornament

St Margaret's Church, St Margaret's, Hereford and Worcs. The rood loft survived the Reformation, although the screen, if there was one, has disappeared.

of their period. In the eighteenth century additional galleries were sometimes inserted over the aisles of a medieval church, to provide more seating space. New churches of this period were often built with integral galleries round the north, south and west walls.

Side galleries were generally removed from medieval churches by the Victorian restorers; they certainly detracted from the architectural character, as can be seen in the few examples where they have survived, such as the church at Whitby, Yorkshire. West galleries were often also removed, the choir and organ being moved down into the body of the church, but a large number remain, sometimes having been used in the nineteenth century for school-children.

Lecterns

Lecterns were either of the desk type — double- or single-sided — or in the form of an eagle or other bird. They were generally of wood, but eagle lecterns were sometimes of brass. Comparatively few have survived in parish churches, having been in most cases superseded after the Reformation by the reading pew. The great majority of existing lecterns are of nineteenth- or twentieth-century date, and in general follow the medieval form. Occasionally we may find a lectern made up of timber from the old reading pew, or even from the base of a vanished screen.

An effigy, probably from the fourteenth century, of a Sherwood forester at St Andrew's Church, Skegby, Notts.

Monuments

The subject of church monuments could fill a book on its own. They can often tell us something of the history of a church, in particular the periods of greatest prosperity in the parish, since the more elaborate monuments were put up by the richer families. We may find a series of monuments to a particular family erected over several centuries.

The earliest medieval monuments were simple stone slabs, inscribed with a cross, and sometimes slightly raised or moulded. From the later twelfth century onwards, sculptured figures — not necessarily accurate portraits of the deceased — became more common. The figures were nearly always shown as if asleep, with the hands joined in prayer, and they are a good source of information on contemporary costume.

Sometimes the figures are set in a recess or niche in a wall, under an arched canopy, but often they are free-standing, lying on a solid base known as a table-tomb. The sides of these are often decorated, either with traceried panels, shields bearing the coats of arms of the deceased, or small kneeling figures of their children, or angels. In later medieval times when there was a great pre-occupation with the thought of death, we sometimes see a richly dressed figure on the top of the tomb, and a cadaver, or skeleton, in a recess below. Stone and alabaster were the most popular materials for monuments at this time, and they were often coloured. Traces of this original colour can still sometimes be seen, but many monuments have been re-coloured in recent times — a matter on which there are strongly differing views. Monumental brasses were another common form of medieval monument, and are also useful sources for costume design. The brasses — cut-out figures, sometimes under canopied niches — were set into stone slabs, or matrices, and often

A brass of 1435, to Thomas Wideville and his wife, at St Owen's , Bromham, Beds.

these slabs are all that is left, the brass itself having been lost or stolen. Brasses were nearly always originally set in the floor, unless they were on top of a table tomb, but many of them have been refixed vertically on walls, to protect them from damage.

After the Reformation monumental sculpture continued to develop, perhaps employing some of the skills of those craftsmen who would previously have produced figures of the saints. In the sixteenth and seventeenth centuries the deceased were often shown kneeling, rather than recumbent, and were sometimes accompanied by smaller figures of their children. Wall monuments now became more common than free-standing tombs, and their designs showed Classical influence. By the eighteenth century the figures of the deceased were often shown in a more lifelike position, and for a time it became popular to depict them in Roman costume. Imported marbles were increasingly used for monuments.

Apart from the sculptured memorials simple inscribed tablets became increasingly common during the eighteenth century, generally of Classical design. The inscriptions are often worth studying, although they may sometimes seem rather fulsome for present-day taste. A particularly interesting collection of these tablets may be studied in Bath Abbey, Avon. In the seventeenth and eighteenth centuries, when Gothic architecture was out of fashion, large monuments were sometimes erected blocking medieval windows and arches, or filling what had once been a chapel. Some of these were moved by later restorers. By the nineteenth century large-scale figure sculpture had become comparatively rare, except for the very wealthy, and tablets were often in a revived Gothic rather than a Classical style.

Although, as we have seen, the quality of the monuments can be a good guide to the periods of prosperity in a parish, we must remember that monuments were often refixed when churches were rebuilt. They can, indeed, be a clue to the fact that a Victorian church has replaced an earlier one, and that it might retain other early features.

Hatchments

Hatchments, although not strictly monuments, are closely related to them. They are painted boards bearing the coats of arms of deceased parishioners entitled to bear them, and were carried in the funeral procession, after which they were often fixed in the church. To the student of heraldry, hatchments can be of great interest, enabling one to tell whether the deceased was a man, a married woman or a spinster and, if married, whether survived by his or her spouse.

The church of Compton Wynyates, Warwicks was rebuilt after being destroyed in the Civil War. The photograph shows the pulpit halfway down the nave, and a block of four hatchments of the family who owned Compton Wynyates House.

The Royal Arms. TOP LEFT *Royal Arms of Elizabeth I, painted on the tympanum at St Mary's Church, Kenninghall, Norfolk.* TOP RIGHT *Royal Arms of Charles I, above a panel of loyal texts, All Saints' Church, Messing, Essex.* BOTTOM LEFT *Carved Royal Arms of Charles II, St Mary's Church, Monnington-on-Wye, Hereford and Worcs.* BOTTOM RIGHT *Royal Arms of Anne, St Mary's , Carisbrooke, Isle of Wight.*

Royal Arms

The Royal Arms began to be displayed in churches in Tudor times, but this became compulsory after the Restoration of King Charles II, as a pledge of loyalty after the Commonwealth. Most royal coats of arms are painted on wooden boards, but we also find examples in carved wood, and occasionally in metal.

Often the initials of the monarch, and occasionally the date, are included in the design and, particularly in the Stuart period, they are

214

further enriched with loyal texts. The designs themselves can be quite unsophisticated, and one suspects that they may be the work of a local painter more used to making inn signs. Occasionally we find that a Royal Arms has been altered to commemorate a new monarch. They became less common in the reign of Queen Victoria, but a few modern examples may be found.

Organs

Small organs were used in some parish churches in the later medieval period, but none of these has survived, and the oldest organs we are likely to find are the eighteenth- and early nineteenth-century barrel organs. These have cylindrical barrels, adapted to play a number of the more popular metrical psalm tunes. Pipe organs were introduced in the eighteenth century, more often in cathedrals than in parish churches, although a few examples of the latter have survived, with cases of attractive Classical design. In the nineteenth century organs became almost universal in churches, and they were often found to be difficult to fit into medieval buildings. Sometimes they were placed in a west gallery, but as chancel choirs became more popular it was usual to move the organ to the east end of the church, where it sometimes blocked a chapel or aisle. Nineteenth-century churches did not generally have this problem, as they were built with specially designed organ chambers. Some of these later organs also have well designed casework.

Miscellaneous

There are a number of other fittings we may sometimes find in old churches, which add to their interest, and can tell us something about their history.

The elaborately carved chest with three locks in St Cuthbert's Church, Kirkleatham, Cleveland dates from the fourteenth century, though the church which houses it was rebuilt in the eighteenth century.

CHESTS Parish churches were required to provide a secure chest in Tudor times, to store the registers and other valuables. They are generally of oak, and often have three locks, only to be opened when the incumbent and both churchwardens were present.

ALMSBOXES These generally date from the seventeenth century onwards, the most popular form being a wooden box on a short column, sometimes inscribed with an appropriate text.

CHARITY BOARDS Boards inscribed with details of local charitable bequests were common in the eighteenth century, and many have survived, although they may have been relegated to the base of the tower, or the vestry. They provide an interesting insight into the social conditions of the time, showing how the Church provided for the care of the old and infirm, and for the education and apprenticeship of orphan children. Some of the charities may still be operative in the parish.

DOLE CUPBOARDS AND SHELVES Another reminder of the 'welfare' functions of the Church may be seen in the form of cupboards or shelves used for putting out loaves of bread or other food for the poor of the parish — sometimes on particular festivals.

GRAVESIDE SHELTERS Occasionally found, and generally in a fairly inconspicuous place in the church, are portable wooden shelters, looking rather like small sentry boxes. They were used in the eighteenth and early nineteenth centuries to provide some shelter for the priest officiating at funerals.

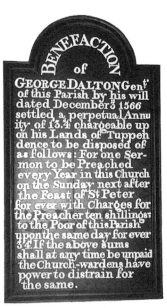

George Dalton's benefaction of 1566, detailed on a charity board (painted at a later date) in St Giles' Church, Farnborough, Kent.

St Mary's Church, Tetbury, Glos. One of the fine brass candelabra of 1781. They were removed during a nineteenth-century restoration, but fortunately were not destroyed, and they have now been reinstated.

BELLS These are rarely accessible to the casual church visitor. A number of churches retain one or more medieval bells, and rather more of the sixteenth, seventeenth and eighteenth centuries. Many, though, were recast in the nineteenth and twentieth centuries. Sometimes an old bell, no longer safe for ringing, may be seen standing on the floor of the church, and these often bear interesting inscriptions.

SWORD AND MACE RESTS These, generally of eighteenth-century date, may be found, particularly in town and city churches. They are nearly always of wrought iron, sometimes incorporating coats of arms. The mace rest may be associated with a special pew for the mayor.

CANDELABRA AND LAMPS Although true 'evening' services were rare until oil, gas, and electric lighting were introduced, many churches have fine eighteenth-century candelabra, generally of brass. Some of these have been converted to take electric lamps. Candles were first succeeded by oil lamps, which were often quite decorative. Many of them were removed when gas or electric lighting was installed, but those which survived are now generally appreciated and preserved, even if they are no longer used.

14

The Story of a Church

Having traced the general history of English church design, considered some of its regional differences, and noted some of the features which can help in dating, let us now look at the development of a typical parish church, serving a small settlement which evolved into a market town.

Our church was built in the twelfth century, possibly replacing a timber Saxon building. It was of cruciform plan, with a low central tower, and a small apsidal sanctuary. The tower was carried on massive piers, with fairly narrow arches leading to the nave, sanctuary and transepts. The windows were round-headed and quite small, probably unglazed at this period, and there were north and south doorways near the west end of the nave, the south doorway being the more richly ornamented. The steeply pitched roof, of simple trussed rafter construction, was thatched, and round the eaves, externally, was a corbel table with carved human and animal heads.

Internally, there was no seating in the nave, and a few benches in the sanctuary. This contained a small stone altar, and there may have been

12th century

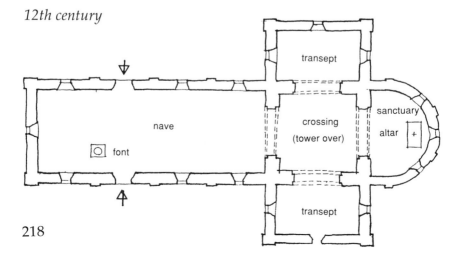

additional altars in the transepts, which were used as chapels. The only furniture in the nave was the font, near the west end. The floor may have been of stone, or perhaps simply of beaten earth, or lime-ash. Lighting was by means of candles or rush lights, and heating, if any, was provided by charcoal braziers. The internal walls were plastered, and covered with coloured decoration, either lined out to represent masonry, or with representations of biblical scenes, mainly in a dark red ochre on a cream ground.

In the thirteenth century the apsidal sanctuary had become too small for the more elaborate ceremonial of the time, and it was taken down and replaced by a new, longer square-ended chancel. At the same time the Norman windows in the east and west transept walls were replaced by new triple lancet windows, admitting more light, and glazed with coloured or 'grisaille' patterned glass. By now the church probably had a stone floor, but there was still no seating in the nave, and the narrow

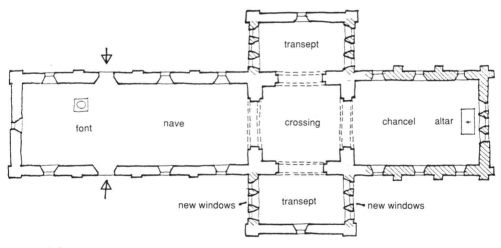

13th century

Norman tower arches formed a definite barrier between the nave and the chancel. The internal walls were still painted, and new designs probably covered the old Norman decorations.

By the early fourteenth century an increase in the population of the parish necessitated an enlargement of the nave, and this was done by building a north aisle, with a lean-to roof. The original north wall was partly removed, to construct an arcade of circular columns with attached shafts and moulded or carved capitals, supporting pointed arches.

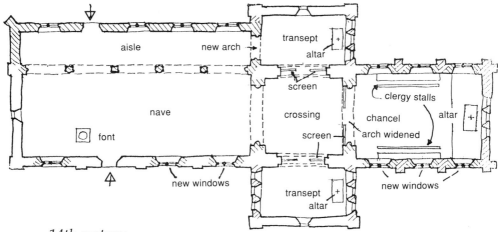

14th century

Another pointed-arched opening was formed linking the new aisle with the north transept. Both the east and west arches to the tower were widened and changed to the pointed form, and a timber screen was constructed, across the eastern arch, to shut off the chancel, as the nave was being used for various secular functions. Screens also separated the crossing from the transept chapels. New, larger traceried windows were inserted in the north and south chancel walls, and in the south wall of the nave. There were still paintings on the walls, including a representation of the Last Judgement over the chancel arch, but the stained glass in the new larger windows was becoming more important as a teaching medium.

In the fifteenth century, when the population of the parish had recovered from the effects of the Black Death and was beginning to share in the prosperity brought about by the growth of the wool trade, further enlargement of the church became necessary. The north aisle was widened to the line of the north wall of the north transept, and a new south aisle of similar width was built. Both of these aisles now had low-pitched lean-to roofs, covered with lead and with battlemented parapets. These aisle roofs were extended to cover the transepts, in place of their old pitched roofs. The thatch on the nave and chancel roofs was replaced by tiling. A new south porch was built, with a store room on its first floor.

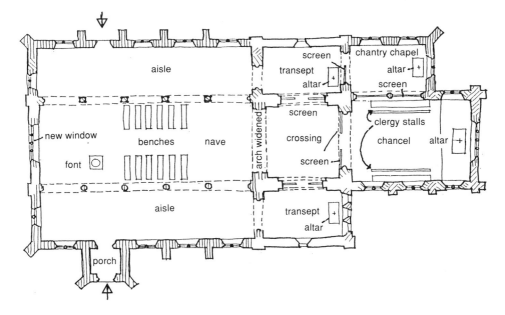

15th century

To the east of the north transept, abutting the chancel, a chantry chapel was built by the local landowner, who provided an endowment to pay a priest to say masses for the souls of members of his family. The main east and west windows of the church were replaced by large new windows in the Perpendicular style, filled with stained glass. A few seats had been provided in the nave, but this was still generally clear of furniture. The chancel had been repaved with encaustic clay tiles. The western tower arch was widened to give a better view of the chancel from the nave.

By about 1500 a major reconstruction had taken place. The local guild of cloth merchants had spent much of their wealth on the church, emulating the rebuilding which had been carried out in an adjoining parish. The alterations previously carried out to the arches of the crossing had weakened the old Norman central tower, and concern for its stability resulted in its being taken down and replaced by an imposing new tower at the west end. The removal of the central tower enabled the east ends of the aisles (the original transepts) to be opened up to the nave, continuing the arcades. The chantry chapel was extended for the full length of the chancel, and a similar chapel, endowed by the merchant guild, was built on the south side of the chancel, served by its own priests. The chapels were given low-pitched roofs, similar to those of the aisles, abutting the

221

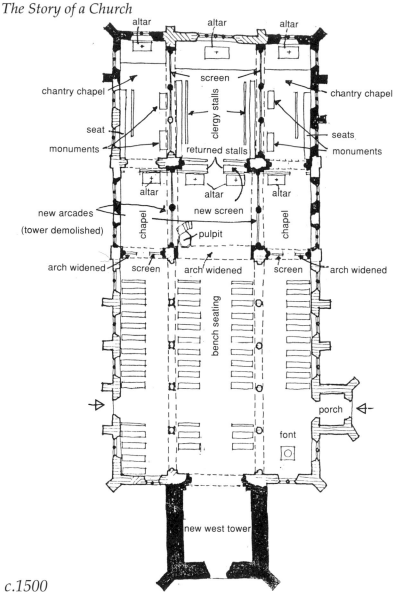

altar

altar

altar

screen

chantry chapel

chantry chapel

clergy stalls

seat

seats

monuments

monuments

returned stalls

altar

altar

altar

new arcades

new screen

(tower demolished)

chapel

chapel

pulpit

arch widened

screen

arch widened

screen

arch widened

bench seating

porch

font

new west tower

c.1500

earlier steeply pitched roof of the chancel. Both chapels contained the tombs of their founding families, and seats for their living members.

The chancel arch was further widened, and a fine new screen, coloured and gilded, surmounted by a loft with a rood, was constructed right across the church, including the two chapels. The loft was used by the

222

choir, who were now providing more elaborate music in addition to the old plainsong. The chancel was fitted out with new stalls, returned against the east face of the screen, and two further altars stood, west of the screen, on each side of its central doorway. The nave now contained a pulpit, in response to the increased importance of preaching, often by visiting friars.

The walls of the nave had been raised, above the arcades, to enable a clerestory to be constructed, and a new low-pitched nave roof was formed, similar to those over the aisles, with ornamental parapets. There were now more seats in the nave, with carved bench ends, but there was still plenty of space around and between the blocks of seating. The increased size of the church reflected not only the growth in population, but an increase in wealth and a desire to provide the parish with the finest church in the district. The interior gave an impression of space, light and colour, very different from the original small, rather dark, Norman church. The church now possessed fine vestments, altar cloths and plate. Statues of the saints looked down from the walls, and the stained glass windows were designed as a sequence round the church, telling the bible story from the Creation to the Last Judgement.

By the early seventeenth century the internal appearance of the church had changed greatly, although there had been no new structural additions or alterations. The chancel screen remained, the figures of the rood, and the loft, having been removed. The chancel stalls also remained, now used by communicants, but the stone altar had been replaced by a wooden table set lengthwise in the chancel. The altars had been removed from the front of the screen and from the side chapels, which now contained family pews and further family monuments.

The nave was seated with box pews, provided and paid for by local families, and fitted with candle sconces. There were a few plain benches in the aisles for visitors, and parishioners who could not afford the pew rents. The fifteenth-century pulpit had been replaced by one fitted with a sounding board, and combined with a reading pew to form a two-decker. The choir was seated in a new west gallery. Some of the stained glass had been replaced by clear glass, but the sheer cost of this had resulted in some of the old windows — those considered to be less 'superstitious' — surviving. The wall paintings had been whitened over, and replaced by panels with biblical texts, and a painted Royal Arms of King James I had replaced the Last Judgement scene over the chancel arch.

Most of the altar cloths, vestments, plate and other treasures had been confiscated in the reign of King Edward VI, leaving only the few things needed for Prayer Book worship. The change in the administration of Communion meant that the old shallow chalices had been replaced by

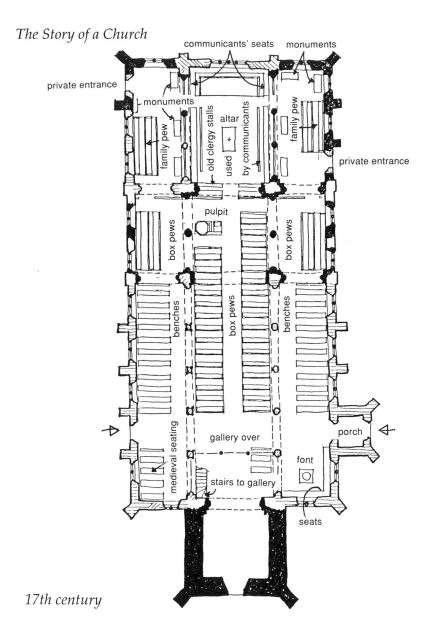

17th century

deeper communion cups and flagons, since all communicants now received the sacrament in both kinds.

By the eighteenth century further changes had taken place. The churchyard now contained a number of gravestones, which had been rare before this time. In the Commonwealth period most of the remaining

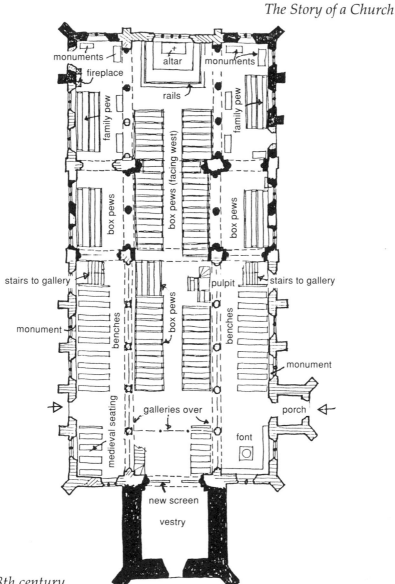

monuments

altar

monuments

fireplace

rails

family pew

family pew

box pews (facing west)

box pews

box pews

stairs to gallery

pulpit

stairs to gallery

monument

benches

box pews

benches

monument

medieval seating

galleries over

porch

font

new screen

vestry

18th century

stained glass had gone, except for a few fragments in the window tracery which had been more difficult to destroy, or more costly to reglaze. The screen had been removed, since the communicants no longer moved into the chancel at the offertory, and more space was needed for seating. Following the Restoration of King Charles II the altar had been moved

225

back to its old position against the east wall and enclosed with rails, but this small sanctuary was rarely used, the Communion being celebrated about four times a year only. Behind the altar were fixed boards inscribed with the Creed, Lord's Prayer and Ten Commandments.

The nave seating had been re-designed to focus on the pulpit, which was now a three-decker, placed halfway down the nave, on one side. The pews to the east of this had been designed to face *west* towards the pulpit. An increase in the population of the parish had made more seating necessary, but rather than enlarge the church, which would have been expensive and resulted in parts of the congregation being too far from the pulpit to hear the sermon, the churchwardens had decided to construct side galleries in the aisles. These were used mainly by children, visitors, and those who could not afford pew rents.

The base of the tower had been screened off to form a vestry, and the choir, accompanied by a barrel organ, still occupied the west gallery. Over the chancel arch a newly painted Royal Arms celebrated the coronation of King George III. Monuments and hatchments to local families covered much of the wall space, and partly blocked some of the windows. Much of the old wall plaster had become dilapidated, and it was covered with a new coat of plaster and limewashed an ochre colour. Although there were still no late evening services the church was now fitted with handsome brass candelabra. The only heating was the fireplace which had been constructed in one of the family chapel pews.

In the mid-nineteenth century a thorough 'restoration' took place. Considerable repairs were carried out to the fabric, and a new vestry, with a boiler room below it, was added to the north side of the north chapel. All the galleries had been removed, and the box pews replaced by open pine benches, free of pew rents. To make up for the loss of the gallery accommodation these new seats were closely packed, leaving only narrow gangways between them. The choir were now seated in the chancel, and as the rows of choirstalls blocked the view of the altar this had been raised on several steps. A new reredos covered part of the base of the east window, and the old Commandment boards had been banished to the base of the tower. The thirteenth-century chancel roof, which had been hidden by a plaster ceiling in the eighteenth century, was renewed in pitch pine.

The south chapel had been cleared of its box pews and some of the monuments, to allow a new altar to be installed, and the chapel furnished for weekday services. The north chapel, however, was used to accommodate a large organ, the space east of this being used as a sacristy. The three-decker pulpit was altered, removing the reading pew and clerk's desk, and reducing it in height. It was then refixed against the

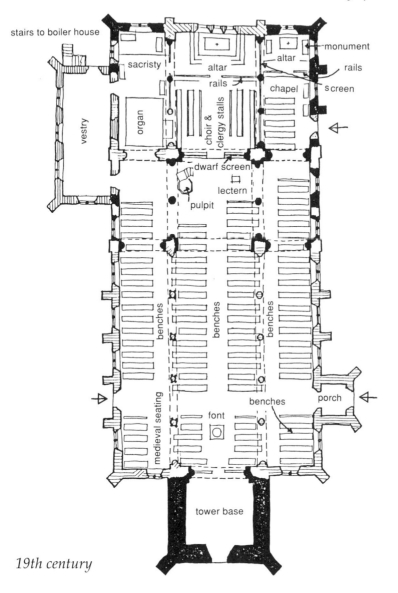

stairs to boiler house

sacristy

altar

monument

altar

rails

rails

chapel

screen

vestry

organ

choir & clergy stalls

dwarf screen

lectern

pulpit

benches

benches

benches

medieval seating

benches

font

porch

tower base

19th century

chancel arch. The priest now read the services from a stall in the chancel.

The construction of the galleries had involved cutting away some of the medieval stonework, and this was now restored. Some of the carved and moulded capitals of the nave arcades, and other stonework which had become rather dilapidated, were renewed. The monuments which had partly covered some of the windows were removed, after considerable arguments with the families concerned. The internal walls were stripped of most of their plaster, and when the eighteenth-century plaster was removed, some of the older layers, with traces of medieval and later paintings, were uncovered. In some parts of the church these were left, but in other areas all the plaster was removed, revealing the bare rubble stonework. The chancel and the gangways in the nave and aisles were paved with new tiling, but the pews were fixed on raised wooden platforms.

Most of the windows were filled with stained glass of varying quality. The main east window, which had been renewed in the fifteenth century, was 'restored' to its thirteenth-century form, from the evidence of some built-up arches in the wall. Some of the more antiquarian-minded members of the parish had wanted to install a new chancel screen, but it was generally felt that this would form too great an obstruction, and a compromise was reached by constructing a stone plinth surmounted by a low wrought-iron screen, with gates. A central heating system had been installed, with large cast-iron pipes run in trenches with gratings, under the floor, and gas lighting brackets had been fixed to the walls.

In the 1960s further changes took place, under the influence of the Liturgical Movement. Several rows of pews were cleared from the east end of the nave, and the altar was brought forward in front of the chancel arch, surrounded by rails on three sides. The choir was moved to the east end of the north aisle, and the chancel refurnished as a Lady Chapel. The south chapel also remained in use, and was enclosed with glass screens to enable it to be separately heated for weekday services and meetings.

To provide more space for processions the rows of pews were shortened, creating wider gangways, and other pews were cleared from the west end of the church to provide more space around the font. In the old chancel and the south chapel the walls which had been stripped of their plaster by the Victorians were replastered and whitened, but the high cost and some local opposition to covering old stone prevented this from being done in the nave.

At the present time more space is needed for social activities, and discussions are taking place in the parish about the relative merits of building a room on to the vestry (which might involve disturbing graves), and screening off one of the aisles, or part of the west end of the church. Any of these schemes will require a faculty, and the negotiations are likely to be prolonged.

From its first foundation in the twelfth century the church has seen many changes, and these are likely to continue as long as it remains in use. Only the Norman font survives, as a reminder of its ancient origin.

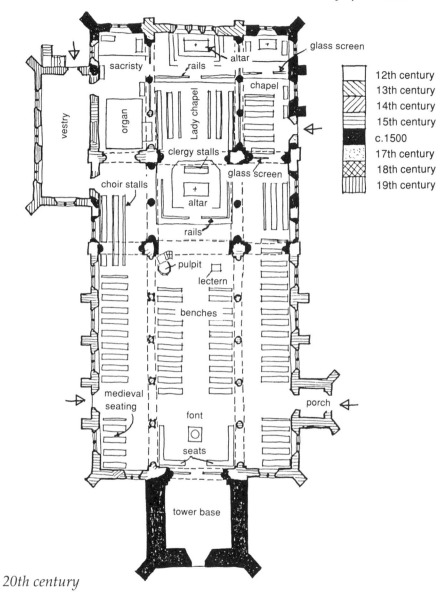

glass screen

sacristy

rails

altar

chapel

vestry

organ

Lady chapel

clergy stalls

glass screen

choir stalls

altar

rails

pulpit

lectern

benches

medieval seating

porch

font

seats

tower base

	12th century
	13th century
	14th century
	15th century
	c.1500
	17th century
	18th century
	19th century

20th century

15

Churches Today

We have seen how churches have survived many changes in religion, politics, and economic and social conditions. About half the Anglican churches in England (8,500 out of a total of about 16,000) are substantially medieval structures — all the more significant a figure when we consider the great increase in the population of the country since the Middle Ages.

What of the future? In some ways the continued survival of our old churches seems more secure than at any time in the past. Apart from popular interest in them as historic buildings, they now probably have more legal safeguards than ever before. One important development was the passing of the Inspection of Churches Measure, 1953, which provides for all Anglican churches to be inspected by an architect or surveyor every five years. Provided always that the recommended repairs are properly carried out, this is doing much to reduce the danger of serious decay as a result of long-term neglect.

On the other hand there can be very real dangers, including population changes and movement, depriving a church of its congregation, and, in some cases, a serious shortage of funds for repairs. No longer is the rector responsible for maintaining the chancel, nor are there the rich landowners who so often paid for church repairs in the past. Side-by-side with a genuine popular interest in ancient buildings is the view put forward in some sections of the Church that money should be spent on other things than repairing church buildings.

Let us look first at the current position relating to the building of, and alterations and repairs to churches. The building of new churches is generally funded jointly by the parish and the diocese, with some help from the Church Commissioners. The repair of existing churches is solely the responsibility of the parish, although grants and loans may be available from the diocese and from various charitable bodies, national and local (see Appendix II). The Directory of Grant-making Trusts, published annually by the Charities Aid Foundation, of 48 Pembury Road, Tunbridge Wells, Kent, includes the names of various grant-making organisations, some of which will help churches. Contrary to popular belief, this work cannot normally be financed by the Church Commissioners, except in the comparatively few cases where, as successor lay rectors, they are responsible for the chancels. Churches of major architectural or historic interest, of all denominations, may be eligible for grants from the Historic Buildings and Monuments Commission for England (English Heritage), and a wider range of churches may receive grants or loans from the local authorities under the Local Authorities (Historic Buildings) Act, 1962. In all these cases, though, the greater part of the cost has to be found by the parish.

If churches are to retain their historic and architectural value it is not enough simply to raise sufficient funds to carry out repairs. These, and any alterations and additions, must be done in a sympathetic manner. We have seen in an earlier chapter how many churches suffered from over-zealous Victorian restoration, and similar mistakes can be made today, causing irreparable damage and loss. What safeguards exist to prevent this?

Many churches, of all denominations, are now included in the *Statutory Lists of Buildings of Special Architectural or Historic Interest*, prepared by the Department of the Environment, but as long as they remain in use for ecclesiastical purposes they are exempt from the normal listed building controls imposed on secular buildings. They are not, however, exempt from *planning* controls, which cover extensions and substantial external alterations. The reasons for the exemption from listed building controls go back to 1913, when it was agreed by the Government that churches would be exempt from the Ancient Monuments legislation on the understanding that the Anglican Church would improve its own machinery to protect its historic buildings, chiefly by establishing Diocesan Advisory Committees for the Care of Churches, consisting of experts in church art and architecture, appointed by the bishop (since 1992, by the Bishop's Council). It was then assumed that only the Church of England possessed buildings of any interest. Anglican churches were already protected to some extent by the Faculty Jurisdiction, which obliged a parish to obtain a faculty (or permit) issued by the Diocesan Chancellor, to carry out any work of demolition, alteration, or addition, including internal furnishings. All faculty applications concerning church buildings, their contents and their curtilage, are examined by the Diocesan Advisory Committees, and although the Diocesan Chancellor is not legally bound to accept their advice, in practice he generally does so. If the proposals involve total or partial demolition he must hold a Consistory Court (the ecclesiastical equivalent of a Public Inquiry), at which any objectors may appear and give evidence. He is also likely to hold a Court if the faculty application is for the sale of an object of great artistic or historic interest, or if the proposal has raised opposition from the Diocesan Advisory Committee or from a large number of objectors.

In general this system works well, but its greatest weakness is the fact that it does not extend to non-Anglican churches, even though the ecclesiastical exemption from listed building control applies to buildings belonging to all religious denominations, regardless of whether they have any equivalent of the Faculty Jurisdiction. In recent years, and linked with the provision of State Aid for historic churches, a start has been made on modifying the ecclesiastical exemption. Non-Anglican churches have been asked to set up their own monitoring system, failing which they may (at least in cases of total or partial demolition) be brought under listed building control. The Department of Christian Life and Worship of the Roman Catholic Church is now recommending the setting up of an Arts and Architecture Committee in each of its dioceses, the equivalent of the Diocesan Advisory Committees in the Anglican Church. Local authorities, and the statutory amenity societies, are to be represented on the Diocesan Advisory Committees. Apart from guarding against unsuitable and over-drastic repairs, the Diocesan Advisory Committees often find themselves having to temper the enthusiasms of certain clergy (perhaps newly-appointed to a parish) who seek to carry out wholesale and sometimes destructive internal alterations in the name of liturgical reform.

One of the greatest risks to the survival of historic churches arises when, because of population movement or economic change, they are no longer needed for worship. Typically these churches are either in remote rural areas or in town centres which have ceased to be residential in character, where in the latter case they may occupy valuable development sites. In this situation there is a difference in the legal position between churches belonging to the Church of England and those of other denominations. In the case of Roman Catholic and Free Churches, a listed church ceases to be exempt from listed building controls once it ceases to be used for ecclesiastical purposes. Planning permission is in any case required for any change of use, and listed building consent will also be needed in these cases for any consequent alterations and, most important, for demolition. If demolition is proposed the final decision will rest not with the local authority, but with the Secretary of State for the Environment, who will first seek the advice of the Historic Buildings and Monuments Commission, and the national amenity societies. The Secretary of State will also have to give the final decision in the case of *alterations* to Grade I and Grade II* buildings, i.e. those of the greatest architectural or historic interest, and he may decide to hold a Public

Inquiry if he considers the case to be of sufficient importance.

The position of the Church of England is quite different. Under the provisions of the Pastoral Measure, 1968, as amended in 1983, and the Redundant Churches Act, 1969, there is a clearly defined procedure for dealing with churches no longer needed for worship. It is not now possible, as it once was, for the Diocesan Chancellor simply to issue a faculty for the demolition of a church, except in cases where a church is to be replaced by a building on the same site, or where demolition is required to comply with a Notice served under the Public Health Acts concerning dangerous structures. In all cases of demolition the chancellor is bound to seek the advice of the Council for the Care of Churches in addition to that of the Diocesan Advisory Committee.

In the case of a redundant church where the above provisions do not apply, the first step is the preparation of a Pastoral Scheme, declaring the church redundant, and this is usually linked with the amalgamation of parishes or livings. A report on the architectural quality and historic interest of the church, its contents and curtilage, must be sought from the Council for the Care of Churches. The local planning authority may comment on the proposal, but cannot prevent it. Once the scheme has been approved by the Privy Council there are three choices for the future of the church, which will be implemented by a Redundancy Scheme. The final decision is taken by the Church Commissioners, who first have to consult the Advisory Board for Redundant Churches on the architectural value of the church. If it is of such interest that its preservation intact with its furnishings is considered desirable, and that any new use would be inappropriate, it is likely to be vested in the Redundant Churches Fund, a body set up under the Pastoral Measure, and funded by both the Church and the State. If, on the other hand, the Board considers that the church is of no architectural merit, or is beyond realistic repair, it may agree to demolition. These provisions apply irrespective of whether or not the church is listed. A new body, the Historic Chapels Trust, corresponding to the Redundant Churches Fund, has recently been set up to care for redundant churches and chapels of other denominations considered to be of sufficient architectural or historic interest.

The majority of churches, though, fall between these two categories, and it is then the responsibility of the diocesan authorities to try to find a suitable new use for the building. As is the case with non-Anglican churches, once a listed church ceases to be used for worship it becomes subject to listed building control, so that any new use will require planning permission, and consequent alterations will need listed building consent as well as the approval of the Church Commissioners and the Advisory Board. If, though, at the end of three years no suitable use has

been found, the Church Commissioners may decide either to vest the church in the Redundant Churches Fund, or to authorise demolition — even if the church is listed — without their having to obtain listed building consent. This is perhaps the most controversial aspect of the present position, and there are signs that it may be modified. If the demolition of a listed church is opposed by the Advisory Board for Redundant Churches, by the local planning authority, or by national amenity societies, a non-statutory Public Inquiry may be held by the Secretary of State, and although the Church Commissioners are not legally bound to accept the inspector's recommendation, demolition in these circumstances is likely to be the exception.

From the implementation of the Pastoral Measure 1968, on April 1st, 1969, until the end of 1991, a total of 1317 Anglican churches were declared redundant. Of these 286 have been preserved intact, mostly by the Redundant Churches Fund, 302 have been demolished, and 729 adapted to new uses. During the same period 430 new churches were opened in England. At present, though one cannot speak for the future, the rate of churches being proposed for redundancy is gradually diminishing.

Churches may become redundant for a variety of reasons. One common situation is that of a church in a town centre which has lost its residential

ABOVE and LEFT *St Mary's Church, Old Dilton, Wilts. This small medieval church was refurnished in the eighteenth century, with box pews and a three-decker pulpit part-way down the nave. It escaped Victorian restoration, as a new church was built at Dilton Marsh, the new centre of population in the nineteenth century. The old church fell into disuse, and is now in the care of the Redundant Churches Fund.*

character, becoming commercial or industrial. Some churches in this situation find new roles in ministering to office or factory workers. In the square mile of the City of London, with its very small resident population, and in spite of nineteenth-century demolitions and losses in the Second World War, there are still over thirty churches in use, some of them having been given a special role as Guild Churches. In Norwich, on the other hand, with its many medieval churches, most of these have been adapted to new uses of varying degrees of appropriateness.

In rural areas it is now becoming more and more common for several parishes to be grouped under one incumbent, some aspects of the 'pluralism' which was regarded as so undesirable in both medieval and Victorian times now being accepted as an unavoidable fact of life. While villages, however small, are generally reluctant to lose their churches, many are being closed. Finding suitable new uses is not always easy, particularly if the churchyard is to remain in use for burials. With a church of any architectural merit, almost any use is preferable to demolition. The latter is final, whereas if the building is retained there is always the possibility that in a changed situation it may one day be

St George's Church, Gravesend, Kent. Repairs in progress in 1969. In the 1950s, following large-scale clearance around the church, it lost its congregation, and was in danger of demolition. However, it was retained because of its historic and architectural interest. In the 1960s, a change in the town plan has resulted in the church becoming once again the main parish church of the town.

restored to its original use. This has happened in the past, as we have seen in the case of the old church at Chingford, Essex, and the Saxon chapel at Bradford-on-Avon, Wiltshire, which was used as a cottage for several centuries before being restored as a church. Many old churches have been through bad periods when their future seemed hopeless. A study of the past history of our churches should give us some hope for the future, although there is no reason for complacency.

Appendix I Glossary

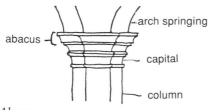

Abacus

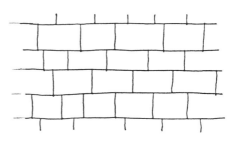

Ashlar stonework

ABACUS A flat slab of stone at the top of a CAPITAL just below the springing of the arch.

ACT OF SUPREMACY The Act of Parliament, passed in 1534, in which King Henry VIII repudiated the authority of the Pope over the Church of England.

AISLE An extension to the side of the NAVE generally separated from it by an ARCADE. Also sometimes used for the gangways between rows of seating.

ALTARPIECE *see* REREDOS

APSE A semi-circular recess, often at the east end of a church, where it forms the SANCTUARY.

APSIDAL Of or like an apse.

ARCADE A range of columns supporting a series of arches.

ARCH-BRACED TRUSS A roof truss where curved braces help to strengthen the tie-beam or collar-beam.

ASHLAR STONE Stone cut into smooth rectangular blocks, laid with fine joints in regular courses.

AUDITORY CHURCH A church planned primarily to enable the congregation to see and hear the preacher.

AUMBRY A recessed cupboard or safe in a church wall, generally in the sanctuary.

BALDACCHINO *see* CIBORIUM

Baluster

BALUSTERS Turned vertical stone or timber members, supporting a handrail or capping.

BARREL ROOF Also sometimes called a waggon roof. A trussed rafter roof, where the rafters have curved braces and are often plastered on the underside, divided into panels by moulded ribs.

Glossary

BASILICA A public aisled hall, in Roman times, used as a model for early churches. (Thus: BASILICAN.)

BAY A longitudinal division in a church; for instance, the distance between the centres of arcade columns, or between roof trusses.

Billet moulding

BILLET A Norman ornamental moulding, consisting of two or more rows of cylindrical blocks, staggered.

BOSSES Carved stones covering the intersections of the ribs of a VAULT.

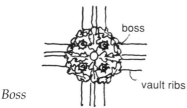

Boss

BOX PEWS High enclosed pews, with doors, introduced after the Reformation.

BRACES Timber members, often curved, linking vertical and horizontal members in a roof, to strengthen the joint between them and help prevent distortion.

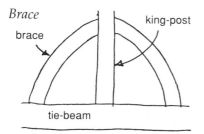

Brace

BROACH SPIRE A form of spire common in the thirteenth century, in which an octagonal spire rises from a square base, with an overhang at the eaves.

CANONS The clergy serving a secular (non-monastic) cathedral, or a collegiate church. May also mean the laws of the Church.

CAPITAL The carved or moulded feature at the top of a column.

CATHEDRAL The principal church of the diocese, containing the seat ('cathedra') of the bishop.

CENTRE A temporary timber structure to support an arch under construction.

CHANCEL The eastern part of a church, normally occupied by the clergy and choir.

CHANTRY An endowment to pay for prayers and masses for the dead.

CHANTRY CHAPEL A chapel built and endowed as a place for chantry prayers and masses.

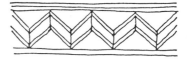

Chevron moulding

CHEVRON A Norman ornamental moulding, of a zig-zag form.

CIBORIUM Sometimes BALDAC-CHINO. A solid canopy over the altar.

CLERESTORY A range of windows lighting the upper part of the nave of a church, above the aisle roof.

CLOISTER An open courtyard surrounded by covered walkways. Typical of monastic churches, they are sometimes found in secular cathedrals.

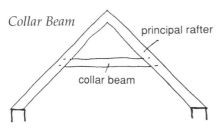

Collar Beam

COLLAR BEAM A beam connecting a pair of principal or common rafters in a roof, at some distance above their feet.

COLLAR PURLIN A longitudinal timber joining a series of collars at their centres in a trussed rafter roof.

COLLEGIATE CHURCH A church served by a college of secular priests or canons, but not the seat of a bishop.

COMMISSIONERS' CHURCHES Churches built in the early nineteenth century, by the State, following the passing of the Church Building Act, 1820.

COMMON RAFTERS Pairs of rafters forming a pitched roof, either supported on purlins and trusses, or framed in a TRUSSED RAFTER ROOF.

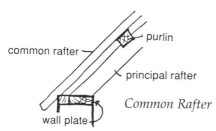

Common Rafter

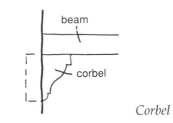

Corbel

CORBEL A projection of stone or timber, carrying the end of a beam, a roof member, or a statue.

CORBEL TABLE A series of carved corbels, round the eaves of a church, typical of Norman work.

CROSSING The space under a central tower, or between the north and south transepts, in a church.

CROWN GLASS Early blown glass, cut from a disc and having a slightly uneven surface.

CRUCIFORM Cross-shaped, as applied to the plan of a church.

CURATE Now generally describes an assistant priest in a parish, but originally it meant the incumbent, who had the 'cure' (or care) of souls.

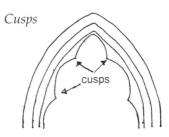

Cusps

CUSPS Pointed curved projections in window tracery or arches.

239

Glossary

DEAN The principal canon on the staff of a secular cathedral, who is responsible for running the cathedral and its services.

DECORATED A term for the second Gothic style, dating from the late thirteenth to the mid-fourteenth century.

DIOCESE An ecclesiastical division of the country, under the supervision of a bishop, and containing a number of parishes.

EARLY ENGLISH A term for the earliest English Gothic style, dating from the late twelfth to the late thirteenth century.

EASTER SEPULCHRE An arched recess, generally on the north side of the sanctuary, where the consecrated bread and the altar cross were kept from Good Friday until Easter Day, before the Reformation.

ECCLESIOLOGY A word coined in the nineteenth century, to mean the study of church art, and the promotion of 'correct' Gothic ideas.

FACULTY A permit to carry out works of alteration to an Anglican church, issued by the Diocesan Chancellor.

FAN VAULT The latest form of English Gothic vaulting, where separate ribs and panels were replaced by solid stone cones (or 'fans') enriched with traceried panelling.

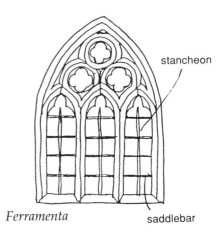

Ferramenta   stancheon   saddlebar

FERRAMENTA The supporting ironwork in a window, to which the leaded glazing is wired.

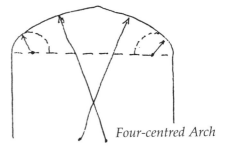

Four-centred Arch

FOUR-CENTRED ARCH An arch struck from four centres, in use from the later fifteenth to the mid-seventeenth centuries, sometimes called a 'Tudor' arch.

FRONTAL A cloth, often embroidered, covering an altar.

Fan Vault

GLEBE Land belonging to the Church, to provide an income for the clergy.

GNOMON The projecting metal arm of a sundial.

GOTHIC ARCHITECTURE The style of architecture, based on the pointed arch, which lasted, in Europe, from the late twelfth century to the mid-sixteenth century, and was revived in the eighteenth and nineteenth centuries.

GRADINE A shelf behind an altar, forming part of the REREDOS.

GRISAILLE GLASS Stained glass, predominantly grey in colour, in geometrical designs, typical of the thirteenth century.

GROINS The intersections between the curved surfaces of vaults.

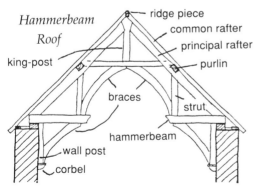

Hammerbeam Roof

king-post, ridge piece, common rafter, principal rafter, purlin, braces, strut, hammerbeam, wall post, corbel

HAMMER-BEAM ROOF The latest form of medieval timber roof, in which the arch-braced principal rafters are carried on cantilevers, known as hammer-beams, helping to reduce the thrust on the walls.

HATCHMENTS Boards painted with coats of arms, carried in funeral processions, and sometimes fixed to the church wall.

IMPROPRIATION The control of a parish church by a monastery, which took the tithes and appointed a vicar, or priest-in-charge.

JAMBS The sides of door or window openings.

KING POST A vertical member in a roof truss, rising from the tie or collar-beam to support the ridge.

LANCETS *or* **LANCET WINDOWS** The tall, narrow pointed-arched windows typical of the early thirteenth century.

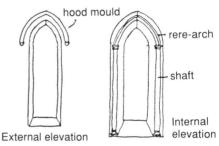

hood mould, rere-arch, shaft, Internal elevation, External elevation, Plan *Lancet Window*

LIERNE RIBS Short ribs in a ribbed vault, connecting the main and

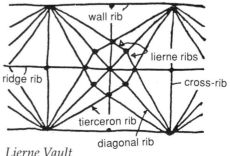

wall rib, lierne ribs, ridge rib, cross-rib, tierceron rib, diagonal rib

Lierne Vault

intermediate ribs, often producing a star-like design.

LISTED BUILDING A building included in the *Statutory Lists of Buildings of Special Architectural or Historic Interest*, issued by the Department of the Environment.

LONG AND SHORT WORK A method of forming quoins, (external angles) in Saxon architecture, consisting of long, narrow blocks of stone placed alternately vertically and horizontally.

LYCHGATE A gate, usually roofed, at the entrance to a churchyard.

MATRIX A stone graveslab, formerly containing a brass, showing the recess for the vanished brass.

MENSA The top member of an altar, of stone or wood.

MISERICORDS Tip-up seating, in a chancel, generally for monks or other clergy.

MULLION A vertical, generally stone, member, dividing a window into sections known as lights.

NARTHEX A large covered porch, or a courtyard, at the west end of an Early Christian church.

NAVE The main body of a church, used by the congregation.

NEWELL A post supporting a stair, or a heavier framing member in an altar rail, sometimes projecting above the rail itself.

NICHE A recess in a wall, often canopied, and sometimes containing, or once containing, a statue.

NORMAN The style of architecture introduced into Britain after the Norman conquest, and dating from the late eleventh to the late twelfth century.

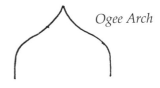
Ogee Arch

OGEE A double or wave-shaped curve, used in mouldings, and as an arch form in window tracery in the fourteenth century.

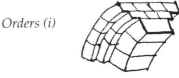
Orders (i)

recessed orders in an arch

ORDERS (i) In Norman and Gothic architecture, the series of recessed stages in an arch, often moulded or carved. (ii) In Classical and Renaissance architecture, the three types of column, Doric, Ionic and Corinthian, governing the design and proportions of Classical buildings.

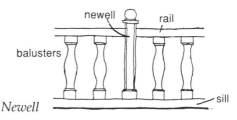
newell · rail · balusters · sill
Newell

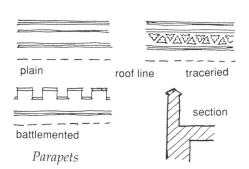

plain roof line traceried

battlemented section

Parapets

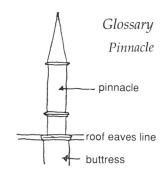

Pinnacle

pinnacle

roof eaves line

buttress

PARAPET A wall extending above a roof, at the eaves or at a gable.

PARISH The smallest ecclesiastical and civil unit.

PARISH CLERK A layman appointed to assist the incumbent in the conduct of the services in a parish church.

PEDIMENT A shallow triangular, or occasionally curved, head to a door or window opening, or at the top of panelling, as in eighteenth-century altarpieces.

Pediment

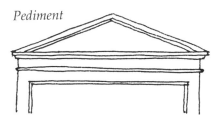

PERPENDICULAR A term for the final phase of English Gothic architecture, dating from the mid-fourteenth to the late sixteenth century.

PILASTER STRIPS Very shallow buttresses, of no structural significance, typical of Saxon work.

PINNACLES Pointed stone vertical projecting members, often found at intervals along a parapet and on a tower, sometimes crowning buttresses.

PISCINA An arched recess in the wall of a church, containing a drain, used for washing the communion vessels.

PLAINSONG An early form of church music, in simple unison.

Poppy-head

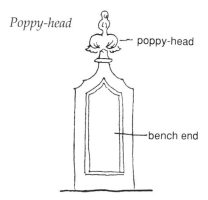

poppy-head

bench end

POPPY-HEAD The shaped top of a bench end.

PORTICUS Lateral projections, or transepts, in a Saxon church.

PROPRIETORY CHAPELS Churches, not serving a parish, but built by 'private enterprise' in the early nineteenth century.

243

Glossary

PRINCIPAL RAFTERS The main rafters in a roof truss, supporting the purlins and ridge.

PURLINS Longitudinal horizontal members in a roof, supporting the common rafters, and themselves carried on the principal rafters.

PYX A vessel, usually of silver, to hold the Reserved Sacrament. In England in medieval times it was often hung in front of the altar.

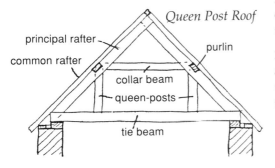
Queen Post Roof

principal rafter
common rafter
purlin
collar beam
queen-posts
tie beam

QUEEN-POST ROOF A roof in which the trusses have two vertical members which support the principal rafters, rising from the tie-beam and generally tied at their heads by a collar-beam.

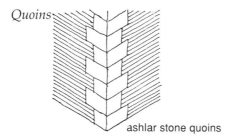
Quoins
ashlar stone quoins

QUOINS The stones forming the external angles in a wall. Also sometimes used to describe the angle itself.

244

RAFTERS The sloping timbers in a roof.

READING PEW A seat in the nave, where the service was read by the priest, after the Reformation.

RECTOR The priest in charge of a parish, entitled to receive the tithes.

RERE-ARCH An internal arch to a gothic window, typical in particular of thirteenth century lancets.

REREDOS *or* **ALTARPIECE** A painted, carved, or panelled feature at the back of the altar.

REVEALS The inner faces of door and window openings, in the thickness of the wall. In thick walls these are often splayed internally.

RIBBED VAULTS Vaults formed by constructing a series of open arches (ribs), with an infilling afterwards laid between them.

RIDDELLS Curtains hung at each end of an altar, at right angles to its length.

RIDGE The highest point of a roof.

RIDGE PIECE *or* **BEAM** A beam forming the ridge of a roof, supporting the tops of the common rafters, and itself supported on the main trusses.

RIDGE RIB A longitudinal rib at the highest point of a vault.

ROMANESQUE The style of architecture derived from Roman, found in Europe from the fifth to the twelfth centuries. Saxon and Norman are forms of Romanesque.

ROOD A large crucifix flanked by figures of Saints Mary and John, at the entrance to the chancel of a church.

ROOD LOFT A loft or gallery at the top of a chancel screen (or rood screen). Occasionally a loft is found fixed directly to the wall between the nave and the chancel, without a screen.

RUBBLE STONE Roughly cut stone in a wall, either random, or laid in courses, with fairly thick mortar joints.

Rubble Walling

coursed

brought to courses

random

SACRISTY A room in a church where the plate and vestments are kept, also often used as a clergy vestry.

SANCTUARY The eastern part of a church, occupied by the altar.

SAXON The style of English architecture, from the conversion of the Saxons to the Norman conquest.

SECULAR As applied to a cathedral, one served by canons or non-monastic priests.

SEDILIA Seats for the clergy, in the chancel, formed as a series of recesses in the south wall.

SEE The area, corresponding to the diocese under the jurisdiction of a bishop, generally identified with the cathedral city.

SHAFTS Small subsidiary columns, surrounding the main columns in an arcade, or adjoining the jambs of a door or window opening.

SHINGLES Thin slabs of timber, usually oak, used in roofing. Most often now found on timber spires.

SPANDRILS or SPANDRELS The spaces between the outside of an arch and its surrounding frame, particularly in a doorway.

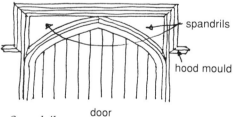

Spandril

door

SQUINT An opening cut, often on the slant, through an internal wall in a church.

STILTS Short vertical sections at the base of an arch, to raise the height of a round arch without increasing the span.

Glossary

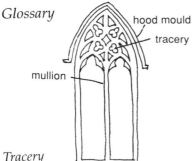

Tracery

STRUT An alternative name for a BRACE, but a term generally used of straight timbers.

TABERNACLE A cupboard or box to hold the Reserved Sacrament, usually standing on the altar or on a shelf behind it, the GRADINE.

THEGN The principal landowner in a parish in Saxon times, corresponding to the later Lord of the Manor.

TIE-BEAM A beam joining the feet of a pair of principal rafters in a roof truss.

TIERCERON RIBS Intermediate ribs in a ribbed vault.

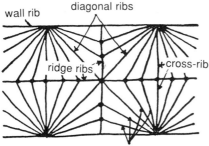

Tierceron Vault

TITHES The tenth part of all produce, in money or in kind, paid to the Church.

246

TRACERY Ornamental stonework in the upper part of a Gothic window.

TRANSEPTS Projecting areas on each side of the nave, often in line with a central tower.

TREE OF JESSE A favourite subject in medieval religious art, showing the descent of Christ from Jesse in the form of a 'family tree'.

TRIFORIUM A gallery over the aisle roof, between the top of the arcade and the CLERESTORY windows. More often found in cathedral and abbey churches than in parish churches.

TRUSS A framed structure supporting a roof, consisting of a pair of principal rafters, secured by a TIE-BEAM or COLLAR-BEAM, supporting purlins, which in turn support the common rafters.

TRUSSED RAFTER ROOF A roof without main trusses, but generally having tie-beams at intervals. Each pair of rafters is joined by a collar. Sometimes there are struts between the collar and the rafters.

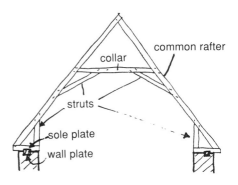

Trussed Rafter Roof

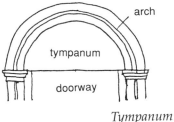

Tympanum

TYMPANUM (i) A slab of stone filling the arch of a Norman or Gothic doorway. (ii) A lath and plaster or boarded partition filling the space between the top of the chancel screen and the chancel arch.

TWO-CENTRED ARCH A pointed arch struck from two centres.

VAULT(i) A stone roof over a church. (ii) A crypt or underground chamber, especially one used for burials.

VICAR A priest in charge of a parish, not entitled to receive the tithes — literally a 'deputy'.

VILLA (ROMAN) A country house, generally the centre of an estate.

VISITATION REPORT (Bishop's or Archdeacon's) A report on the state of a parish, including its buildings, prepared periodically by the bishop or archdeacon.

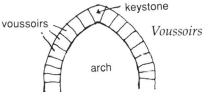

Voussoirs

VOUSSOIRS The individual stones, generally tapered, making up an arch.

WAGGON ROOF *see* BARREL ROOF

Appendix II Organisations concerned with churches

ADVISORY BOARD FOR REDUNDANT CHURCHES Fielden House, Little College Street, London SW1 *A body of specialists in church art and architecture, appointed under the Pastoral Measure to advise the* CHURCH COMMISSIONERS *on the future of redundant Anglican churches. Publishes an annual report.*

BARRON BELL FUND c/o Managing Trustees, 16 Horse Grove Avenue, Ticehurst, East Sussex *Gives grants for re-hanging and restoring existing peals of church bells.*

CATHEDRALS ADVISORY COMMISSION FOR ENGLAND 83 London Wall, London EC2M 5NA *Gives advice to the Deans and Chapters on alterations to the fabric, fittings and furnishings of English cathedrals.*

CHAPELS SOCIETY c/o Council for British Archaeology, The King's Manor, York YO1 2EP *Founded to promote the study and survival of Non-Conformist and Roman Catholic churches in Britain.*

CHASE CHARITY 34 North End Road, London W14 OSH *A charity which may give grants for the repair of historic churches.*

CHURCH COMMISSIONERS FOR ENGLAND 1 Millbank, London SW1 *The Commissioners manage the historic endowments of the Church of England, to be used to help pay, house and provide pensions for the clergy. They may also assist in the building of new churches, and they are responsible for making the final decisions on the future of redundant Anglican churches.*

CHURCH MONUMENT SOCIETY The Armouries, H.M. Tower of London, London EC3 *Founded for the study, care and conservation of church monuments, including sculptures, tablets, stained glass and wall paintings associated with burials.*

COUNCIL FOR THE CARE OF CHURCHES 83 London Wall, London EC2M 5NA *The co-ordinating body for the Diocesan Advisory Committees. Publishes booklets on church art and architecture, and an annual report. It is required to prepare a report on all Anglican churches proposed for redundancy. May give grants for the repair of important church furnishings and fittings.*

ECCLESIOLOGICAL SOCIETY 1 Cornish House, Otto Street, London SE17 3PE *Successor to the Cambridge Camden Society which was originally founded in 1840 to promote the study of church art and architecture. The* original society was concerned with the revival of Gothic architecture, and was largely a propaganda body. In its present form the society publishes pamphlets on various aspects of church art and design.

FRIENDS OF FRIENDLESS CHURCHES 12 Edwardes Square, London W8 OHG *May give grants for the repair of historic churches in England and Wales, particularly for those in difficult circumstances.*

GEORGIAN GROUP 37 Spital Square, London E1 6DY *Originally a sub-committee of the* SOCIETY FOR THE PROTECTION OF ANCIENT BUILDINGS, *now a separate organisation concerned with eighteenth-century buildings.*

HISTORIC BUILDINGS AND MONUMENTS COMMISSION FOR ENGLAND (ENGLISH HERITAGE) Fortress House, 23 Savile Row, London W1X 2HE *A Government-funded body concerned with the preservation of historic buildings and monuments. Prepares Lists of Buildings of Special Architectural or Historic Interest for the Department of the Environment. Gives grants to buildings of outstanding interest, and other historic buildings in conservation areas, including churches of all denominations, in use for worship.*

The corresponding bodies for other parts of Britain are:

HISTORIC BUILDINGS AND MONUMENTS DEPARTMENT OF SCOTLAND 3-11 Melville Street, Edinburgh EH3 7RN

HISTORIC BUILDINGS COUNCIL FOR WALES Brunel House, 2 Fitzalan Road, Cardiff CF2 1UY

HISTORIC MONUMENTS AND BUILDINGS BRANCH, DEPARTMENT OF THE ENVIRONMENT FOR NORTHERN IRELAND Calvert House, 23 Castle Place, Belfast BT1 1FY

HISTORIC CHAPELS TRUST c/o 8 Kensington Gate, London W8 5NA. *A body financed by English Heritage to care for redundant churches and chapels of denominations other than the Church of England – corresponding to the Redundant Churches Fund.*

HISTORIC CHURCHES PRESERVATION TRUST Fulham Palace, London SW6 *A charity which makes grants towards the repair of historic churches, of all denominations. There are also local historic churches trusts in many counties.*

INCORPORATED CHURCH BUILDING SOCIETY Fulham Palace, London SW6 *A society founded in 1818 to make grants for the building, repair and enlarging of churches. At the present time it makes interest-free loans only, to Anglican churches in England and Wales, irrespective of their historic or architectural interest.*

Organisations concerned with Churches

LECHE TRUST Christ Church, Spitalfields, Commercial Street, London E1 6LY *Gives grants for repairing church furnishings and fittings, particularly those of the Georgian period.*

REDUNDANT CHURCHES FUND *89 Fleet Street, London EC4Y 1DH. A body set up under the Pastoral Measure to hold and maintain redundant Anglican churches of architectural or historic interest for which no other use is appropriate. It receives funds both from the Church and the State, and can accept private donations. Churches vested in the Fund remain consecrated buildings and can be used for occasional services. The fund is in the process of receiving a new name.*

ROYAL COMMISSION ON HISTORICAL MONUMENTS OF ENGLAND *Alexander House, 19 Fleming Way, Swindon, Wilts SN1 2NG. A government body, appointed to prepare records of historic buildings and monuments. These were originally prepared on a county basis, but now tend to concentrate on smaller areas. The volumes contain detailed descriptions of churches, often with dated plans (see Bibliography).*

SHARPE TRUST c/o the Grant Secretary, Beech Pike, Elkstone, Gloucestershire *Gives grants for re-hanging and restoration of existing bells in churches in England and Wales.*

SOCIETY FOR THE PROTECTION OF ANCIENT BUILDINGS 37 Spital Square, London E1 6DY *A society founded in 1877 by William Morris, to try to prevent the worst excesses of Victorian restoration, particularly of churches. Prepares technical advice on the repair of historic buildings. Organises conferences and courses on this subject and awards annual scholarships. May advise on sources of financial help.*

VICTORIAN SOCIETY 1 Priory Gardens, London W4 *Originally a sub-committee of the Society for the Protection of Ancient Buildings. Now an independent organisation concerned with nineteenth- and early twentieth-century buildings.*

WILLIAM AND JANE MORRIS FUND c/o Assistant Secretary, Society of Antiquaries, Burlington House, London W1V OHS *Gives small grants and loans for the repair of ancient churches and their fittings.*

The City Livery Companies of London may give grants for repairs to churches and their contents, particularly those related to their particular interests.

Local historical and archaeological societies may have records of churches in their areas.

Bibliography

There are many books on church architecture. The following list is a selection, including some concerned with the effect on church design of changes in their use, as well as those in architectural style.

Addleshaw and Etchells *The Architectural Setting of Anglican Worship* London, 1948.

Anderson, M.D. *History and Imagery in British Churches* London, 1971.

Anson, Peter F. *Fashions in Church Furnishings* Leighton Buzzard, 1960.

Atkinson, T.D. *Local Style in English Architecture* London, 1947.

Batsford and Fry *The Cathedrals of England* London, 1938.

— *The Greater English Church* London, 1940.

Betjeman, J. (ed) *Collins Guide to Parish Churches of England and Wales* London, 1980.

Bettey, J. *Church and Parish* London, 1987.

Bond, Francis *Gothic Architecture in England* London, 1906.

Briggs, Martin S. *Goths and Vandals* London, 1952.

Chalford, Mark *Churches the Victorians Forgot* Ashbourne, 1989.

Clarke, Basil *Church Builders of the Nineteenth Century* London, 1938.

Clifton-Taylor, A. *The Cathedrals of England* London, 1967.

— *English Parish Churches as Works of Art* London, 1974.

Cobb, Gerald *The Old Churches of London* 1942.

— *English Cathedrals, the Forgotten Centuries* London, 1980.

Cox and Ford *Parish Churches of England* London, 1937.

Crossley, F.H. *Timber Building in England* London, 1951.

— *The English Abbey* London, 1935.

Ditchfield, P.H. *Parish Clerk* London, 1935.

Dymond, David *Writing a Church Guide* London, 1986.

Foster, Richard *Discovering English Churches* London, 1981.

Harvey, John *Gothic England* London, 1947.

Hole, Christina *English Shrines and Sanctuaries* London, 1954.

NADFAS (Church Recorders Group) *Inside Churches. A Guide to Church Furnishings* London, 1989.

Bibliography

Pevsner, N. *The Buildings of England* (County Series) 1951 seq.
Platt, Colin *The Parish Churches of Medieval England* London, 1981.
Powys, A.R. *The English Parish Church* London, 1936.
Randall, Gerald *The English Parish Church* London, 1982.
Rodwell, Warwick *The English Heritage Book of Church Archaeology* London, 1989.
Sitwell, Sacheverell *British Architects and Craftsmen* London, 1946.
Summerson J. *Georgian London* London, 1988.
Whiffe, Marcus *Stuart and Georgian Churches* London, 1948.

Volumes of the *Survey of the Royal Commission on Historical Monuments of England*. The following counties and smaller areas, containing descriptions of churches, have been published to date: Buckinghamshire, City of Cambridge, West and North-east Cambridgeshire, Dorset, Essex, Herefordshire, Hertfordshire, Huntingdonshire, Stamford (Lincolnshire), London, Middlesex, Churches and Archaeological Sites in Northampton, Architectural Monuments in Northamptonshire, City of Oxford, Westmorland, City of Salisbury, City of York, Saint Alban's Cathedral, Sherborne Abbey (Dorset), York Minster, Historic Buildings in the Central Area of York, Non-conformist Chapels and Meeting Houses in Central England, Churches of South-East Wiltshire, Stained Glass in England 1180–1540, Beverley. Non-conformist Chapels and Meeting Houses in South-West England, Islington Chapels, Whitehaven 1660 to 1800.

Most of these surveys were prepared before the re-organisation of local government in 1974, and are published under the old county names and boundaries. In the earlier surveys no buildings later than 1715 were included. In later surveys the date limit is 1850.
Survey of London Formerly published by the Greater London Council, this is being continued by the Royal Commission on Historical Monuments. The following volumes have been published to date, and contain descriptions of churches:

I *Bromley-by-Bow*
II *Chelsea* Part I
III *Saint Giles-in-the-Fields* Part I: Lincoln's Inn Fields
IV *Chelsea* Part II
V *Saint Giles-in-the-Fields* Part II
VI *Hammersmith*
VII *Chelsea* Part III: The Old Church
VIII *Saint Leonard, Shoreditch*
IX *Saint Helen, Bishopsgate*
X *Saint Margaret, Westminster* Part I

XI *Chelsea* Part IV: The Royal Hospital

XII *All Hallows, Barking-by-the-Tower* Part II

XIII *Saint Margaret, Westminster* Part II: Neighbourhood of Whitehall, Vol.I

XIV *Saint Margaret, Westminster* Part III: Neighbourhood of Whitehall, Vol.II

XV *All Hallows, Barking by the Tower* Part II.

XVI *Saint Martin in the Fields* Part I: Charing Cross

XVII *Saint Pancras* Part I: Village of Highgate

XVIII *Saint Martin-in-the-Fields* Part II: The Strand

XIX *Saint Pancras* Part II: Old Saint Pancras and Kentish Town

XX *Saint Martin-in-the-Fields* Part III: Trafalgar Square and Neighbourhood

XXI *Saint Pancras* Part III: Tottenham Court Road and Neighbourhood

XXII *Saint Saviour and Christ Church, Southwark* Bankside

XXIII *Saint Mary, Lambeth* Part I: South Bank and Vauxhall

XXIV *Saint Pancras* Part IV: Kings Cross and Neighbourhood

XXV *Saint George the Martyr and Saint Mary, Newington, Southwark, Saint George's Fields*

XXVI *Saint Mary, Lambeth* Part II: Southern Area

XXVII *Christ Church and All Saints, Spitalfields and Mile End New Town*

XXVIII *Hackney* Part I: Brooke House

XXIX, XXX *Saint James, Westminster* Part I: South of Piccadilly

XXXI, XXXII *Saint James, Westminster* Part II: North of Piccadilly

XXXIII, XXXIV *Saint Anne* Soho.

XXXV *The Theatre Royal, Drury Lane, and The Royal Opera House, Covent Garden*

XXXVI *The Parish of Saint Paul, Covent Garden*

XXXVII *Northern Kensington*

XXXVIII *The Museums Area of South Kensington and Westminster*

XXXIX *The Grosvenor Estate in Mayfair* Part I: General History.

XL *The Grosvenor Estate in Mayfair* Part II: Buildings

XLI *South Kensington, Brompton*

XLII *South Kensington, Kensington Square to Earls Court*

XLIII *All Saints', Poplar* (in preparation, 1989)

Note The names of these volumes refer to the old London *parishes*, not simply to the churches. Most of these parishes have been sub-divided, and contain several further churches.

INDEX

Page numbers in italics refer to illustrations.

Index